The Jesus Revolution

Learning from Christ's First Followers

LEITH ANDERSON

Abingdon Press
Nashville

THE JESUS REVOLUTION
LEARNING FROM CHRIST'S FIRST FOLLOWERS

Library of Congress Cataloging-in-Publication Data

Anderson, Leith, 1944
   The Jesus revolution : learning from Christ's first followers / Leith Anderson.
      p. cm.
   Includes bibliographical references.
   ISBN 978-0-687-65398-0 (pbk. : alk. paper)
   1. Bible. N.T. Acts—Criticism, interpretation, etc.   I. Title.
   BS2625.52.A53 2009
   226.6'06—dc22

2009017404

09 10 11 12 13 14 15 16 17 18—10 9 8 7 6 5 4 3 2 1

MANUFACTURED IN THE UNITED STATES OF AMERICA

CONTENTS

iii

Contents

PREFACE

At the time of Jesus' death two thousand years ago, a scant 120 Jesus followers lived in the city of Jerusalem—an insignificant number, considering that the estimated Jewish population of Palestine was about four million. Christians (though they wouldn't be called that for a long while) were hardly noteworthy. Outside of causing some dissention among the religious establishment in the area, they had made little measurable impact on the culture or the wider world.

Today, there are about two billion self-identified Christians worldwide,[1] comprising around one-third of our world's population. To say that Jesus and his followers have changed the world would be an absurd understatement. Christians have made enormous change in the world, not just by their numbers, but also by what they believe and how they live.

The book of Acts provides a succinct description of the early days of the faith and it is there that Christians can turn to discover the roots of their own beliefs and behavior. What was different about these believers? Do modern Christians follow the model established by the first believers, many of whom knew Jesus as a friend and mentor? What can we learn by studying their lives, work, and words? How can Christians continue changing the world in positive ways that improve the lives of others and give people hope as Jesus instructed?

Jesus' ministry on earth seeded the Christian faith. We can read Acts as a fascinating historical record, but, better yet, we can allow ourselves to be transformed and deepened in our God-given purpose on earth.

CHAPTER 1

MOVING FORWARD

(ACTS 1:1-11)

For the eleven remaining disciples, a golden era had come abruptly to an end. During the past three-and-a-half years, their teacher, Jesus, had walked with them through countryside, desert, and city, getting his feet as dusty and calloused as their own. He had laughed with them. He had spoken of deep spiritual issues that challenged their assumptions, opened their eyes, and altered their behavior. He had prayed with and for them. And now, suddenly, he was gone.

Jesus had already surprised them once. After hours of brutal torture and a long, lingering death by crucifixion, their teacher had—after three days—risen from death. Stretching out his hands, with nail holes still evident, he had appeared to them while they were locked away in stunned mourning. I imagine the disciples weeping with joy, hugging one another. Their rabbi was alive.

For forty glorious days it was as if he had never left. Acts 1:3 says he continued to serve as their teacher, speaking about the kingdom of God. This had been a central theme through the years, but his disciples still didn't get it. They thought "kingdom" meant an earthly government with a border, capital city, army, and laws, but that wasn't it at all. Jesus' "kingdom of God" referred to people living out God's will on earth. Jesus was calling his followers to a radically different way of living—one of love instead of hate,

1

salvation instead of condemnation, forgiveness instead of revenge. He issued this radical call one last time, wanting them to understand that they were to pursue the kingdom of God—not the kingdoms of earth.

One day he shared a meal with them and instructed them not to leave Jerusalem. Instead, they were to "wait for the gift my Father promised, which you have heard me speak about. For John baptized with water, but in a few days you will be baptized with the Holy Spirit" (1:4b).

These were new ideas for the men.

Not long after this bewildering pronouncement, Jesus called the group together again. There was something in the air. Anticipation. Urgency. Jesus told them they couldn't know God's timetable for the future of political Israel but they could depend on receiving the Holy Spirit very soon—in just ten more days.

"It is not for you to know the times or dates the Father has set by his own authority," he said. "But you will receive power when the Holy Spirit comes on you; and you will be my witnesses in Jerusalem, and in all Judea and Samaria, and to the ends of the earth" (1:7-8).

The Holy Spirit would give them supernatural power to live out the Christian life. The Spirit would reside inside of them, guiding, encouraging, instructing, and blessing them. But they would be given a job to do with the Spirit's help. They would become the messengers of God.

Acts 1:8 contains one of the most important statements by Jesus in the New Testament: "you will be my witnesses." Being a Christian has responsibilities as well as privileges. Being a witness means telling what we have experienced as followers of Jesus the Christ. Being a witness may be difficult and come at a high price. (The Greek word for witness is *martus,* from which comes the English word "martyr.") Christians would be international in relationships—no longer identified by citizenship in a specific nation but part of the family of God in the whole world.

This is the blueprint for Christians to change the world for God—from their hometown to province to neighbor nation to the whole globe. From the moment Jesus gave instructions to his disciples, the gospel of the Christ would begin spreading from Jerusalem to the rest of the world. It would be possible because of the Holy Spirit, not armies, laws, politics, power, fame, or money. The power of Jesus' cause would be spiritual and supernatural. Then something amazing happened. While his followers watched, Jesus physically lifted from the ground, was encompassed in a cloud, and disappeared. There were no protracted good-byes and no time to adjust to this new reality before it occurred. He had returned to heaven and his disciples were alone.

Picture those devoted men standing with their heads tilted back, watching the spot where their Lord and trusted rabbi had vanished into a mist of white. What were they thinking? Jesus had given them very specific instructions for their future work and they were filled with joy that they now understood his purpose, but they must have felt a deep sense of loss—their best friend had been taken away. Again.

Here's what they knew: the Son of God had become human and lived a sin-free life among them. He had died, and through this death he had paid for all human sin—past, present, and future. He had risen from death to live again. And now he had returned to heaven. His job on earth was done. Complete. Jesus' life and ministry on earth were over.

Yet first-century historian and physician Luke explodes that assumption with the first startling words of his second book, the book of Acts: "In my former book, Theophilus, I wrote about all that Jesus began to do and to teach until the day he was taken up to heaven" (1:1-2). [1]

"*Began* to do and to teach." What does that mean? Is Luke saying that the stories of Jesus—from his birth in the most humble of settings to the passionate teaching to the miracles to his ascension—are only the beginning?

To make certain the disciples comprehended the meaning of the event they had witnessed, two angels suddenly materialized, most certainly startling and paralyzing even these men who had seen countless supernatural events during their time with Jesus.

"Men of Galilee,...why do you stand here looking into the sky? This same Jesus, who has been taken from you into heaven, will come back in the same way you have seen him go into heaven" (1:11).

Jesus was not abandoning his followers. He was leaving them for an indeterminate amount of time with a job to accomplish. He promised to return. So Acts is the book that tells us what happened after the disciples left that hilltop. No longer were Jesus' followers staring upward, they were looking forward. It is the book where Jesus' work continues through his followers.

Acts is also the book that carries us—his current believers—into our future. It is where we learn that Jesus cannot be contained in a history of thirty-three years on an ancient strip of land along the eastern shore of the Mediterranean Sea. Acts helps us see that he is still at work in our world.

This is a breathtaking revelation because it includes us. Have you ever wished that you could have followed Jesus? Seen him walk on water? Watched as he healed people's bodies with a touch or a word? Luke's writings in Acts tell us that even as twenty-first–century believers we can experience the presence and power, teaching and ministry of Jesus. Jesus is just getting started. He has much more to accomplish. More miracles. More transformed lives. More of everything he started.

How does this apply to you and me? Like the disciples, we have to get on board. We have to grasp the power and potential that Jesus puts in our hands through the help of the Holy Spirit. We have to accept the call. The book of Acts is a historical record of the early church but it is also a challenge to modern-day Christians. By reading about the activities, worship, beliefs, and behavior of the earliest followers of Jesus recorded in Acts, we see how the church changed the world and how we can be changed, too.

After leaving his disciples, Jesus returned to a place we can only imagine, heaven. There he could represent us to God, build future residences for his followers to live, and command his worldwide endeavor. While living on earth as a human being, Jesus was in only one place at a time. Now the Spirit could be everywhere at once. It was God's excellent plan and it has everything to do with us.

Reflect and Discuss

1. What are your assumptions about the early believers? How were they different from present-day Christians?

2. "No longer were they staring upward, they were looking forward." How does this statement about the first Jesus followers apply to Christians today?

3. How is your view of being a witness similar to or different from that of the first followers?

SEEKING GOD'S WILL

(ACTS 1:12-26)

D
azed but bursting with the news that they had seen Jesus
ascending to heaven from the Mount of Olives, the disciples returned to Jerusalem, a three-quarter-mile walk.
They must have felt conspicuous as they made their way through
the streets. Looking at this scene through modern eyes, I find
myself wondering why they stuck together. The political and religious leaders of Jerusalem were agitated and on high alert, and
they had shown themselves to be unpredictable. Bands of roving
Jesus followers would certainly attract hostile attention, especially just weeks after furious mobs demanded Jesus' arrest and
execution. The disciples may have understood that they would be
safer if they dispersed silently and furtively but something made
them cling to each other.

This began a period of "in-between"—after Jesus had left
them, but before the coming of the Holy Spirit he had promised
them. "In-between" is seldom a comfortable place to
be. Remember your own in-between times: in-between jobs,
houses, relationships, medical appointments. In-between is where
we experience uncertainty, uneasiness, grief, and anxiety. Jesus'
followers—his dearest friends—found themselves unexpectedly
in this unsettling situation with only one another for comfort.
After three years, Jesus—their companion and mentor—would be
absent from their gatherings. They would have to unlearn the

automatic way they turned to him when a question arose. They could no longer grasp his arm for simple reassurance. Although they now knew he had risen from death, seeing him disappear from their view into heaven felt like a physical loss. The disciples had unexpectedly begun living in-between—but not without hope, since their Lord had promised a special gift, the Holy Spirit. So they waited. That first meeting must have been crowded:

> When they arrived, they went upstairs to the room where they were staying. Those present were Peter, John, James and Andrew; Philip and Thomas, Bartholomew and Matthew; James son of Alphaeus and Simon the Zealot, and Judas son of James. They all joined together constantly in prayer, along with the women and Mary the mother of Jesus, and with his brothers. (1:13-14)

They prayed. Everything else had been stripped from them—their security, their peace of mind, their deep friendship with Jesus. Yet God had promised not to abandon them. He was their only hope. Instinctively they knew that prayer with other believers would be their greatest comfort during the days ahead. Those early disciples needed each other. So they prayed.

What did the people pray about? Certainly they cried out their loneliness for Jesus. They prayed that they would be ready when the Holy Spirit came as promised. It can be assumed they prayed for each other, their families, friends, health, work, finances, relationships, and world concerns. And they may have been overflowing with questions. *What should we do, Lord? What is the purpose of our lives now? We want to work for you—but how?*

So they began their in-between period as individuals "all joined together constantly in prayer." They didn't literally pray nonstop without eating or sleeping. The Greek imperfect tense for the word "constantly"[1] means that they were persistent. They kept coming back to pray, to seek God's will, and to follow it. They did this through consultation with the Scriptures.

The remaining followers of Jesus stayed committed, honoring the disciples as their leaders, and selecting Peter as chief among them. It is surprising that Peter is the man put in charge. Remember that Peter was the disciple who had most vehemently and publicly denied Jesus before the crucifixion. Wouldn't this action have disqualified him from leadership of Jesus' remaining flock? It didn't. Jesus had forgiven Peter, and the others responded with mercy too. Why? They forgave because they had known him for years and judged him to be a man of faith and character, despite his flaws. They knew he was deeply committed to Jesus and there must have been agreement that he take the lead.

There was one significant absence in this meeting—Judas, the disciple who had betrayed not only Jesus but also his closest, most trusting friends, the other disciples. Yet Peter spoke about him with amazing respect. His words were measured and full of grace for the man who had given Jesus over to the authorities and to a horrible death. Peter remembers Judas as someone who "served as guide for those who arrested Jesus—he was one of our number and shared in this ministry" (1:17).

At this point, Luke inserted a parenthetical explanation for future readers of this account. Peter didn't need to explain what happened to Judas because everyone in that crowd already knew.

(With the reward he got for his wickedness, Judas bought a field; there he fell headlong, his body burst open and all his intestines spilled out. Everyone in Jerusalem heard about this, so they called that field in their language Akeldama, that is, Field of Blood.) (1:18-19)

Peter's message continued:

"For," said Peter, "it is written in the book of Psalms,
    'May his place be deserted;
        let there be no one to dwell in it,'
and,
    'May another take his place of leadership.' " (1:20)

From his words we see that Peter had spiritually matured through the influence of Jesus and the intense experiences following his death and resurrection. He was conscious of the needs of the others. Helping them make sense of their current situation, Peter quoted Psalm 69:25, paraphrasing the words of the scripture to augment his point. It was more important to get at the truth of the passage than to quote the exact words. He reminded his listeners that the vacancy left by Judas had been described a thousand years earlier. For the people in that meeting, this was no mere historical study; it was to help them accept all that had happened as part of a plan. Peter again found truth to guide them, this time in Psalm 109:8: "May another take his place of leadership."

With a biblical foundation, he now turned to reason and common sense in establishing the criteria for choosing a church leader.

> "Therefore it is necessary to choose one of the men who have been with us the whole time the Lord Jesus went in and out among us, beginning from John's baptism to the time when Jesus was taken up from us. For one of these must become a witness with us of his resurrection." (1:21-22)

His point was simple. They needed a leader with a proven track record of faithfulness over the long haul. Peter also made it a requirement for the next apostle to have witnessed the resurrection of Jesus. No secondhand faith. No uncertainty. He had to have seen and believed firsthand. "So they proposed two men: Joseph called Barsabbas (also known as Justus) and Matthias" (1:23).

Both men had already passed muster by the group as a whole, so now what? How were they to decide between the two? Imagine yourself in a similar position. You have two great job offers, two fabulous individuals who want to marry you, or two different churches to join. It's wonderful to get a choice between two good possibilities but it can also be overwhelming and confusing. Beyond your own preferences, how can you know which one God wants? How do you find God's will?

All 120 again turned to prayer. Would it be Joseph or Matthias? "They prayed, 'Lord, you know everyone's heart. Show us which of these two you have chosen to take over this apostolic ministry, which Judas left to go where he belongs' " (Acts 1:24-25).

I love the line "Lord, you know everyone's heart." The Greek word is *kardiagnostes,* which combines the words for "heart" and "know." In other words, God is the "heart knower." That's a good reminder for how we should pray when taking a job, hiring an employee, voting for elected officials, and a lot of other choices in life. "God, look at our hearts and the hearts of others to choose the right people for leadership."

What happened next seems very strange to modern Christians. They did an equivalent of a coin toss—heads or tails. The Bible says that they "cast lots." The two names were written on stones, the stones were placed in a container, and the container was shaken until a stone came out. Whichever name emerged first decided the question.

And the man was Matthias.

Perhaps the point here is that the people had done everything they knew to do to make the right choice. They had set criteria, used reason, and prayed. With both men still looking equal in qualifications and appeal, they took the last step and made a decision based on what looked like chance. To them, this wasn't strange. Casting of lots was how officials were chosen in the Jerusalem temple. They were convinced that Scripture, reason, and prayer were their responsibility but the ultimate outcome was up to Jesus.

A few days later the Holy Spirit came to these early Christians. After that, there is no record of them ever rolling the stones to make another decision.

Did they get it right? Was the correct decision made? Some critics point out that Matthias is never mentioned again in the Bible and that we know little if anything more about him. They criticize the apostles and early Christians for the process they used and the decision they made. There has always been and always will be controversy and differences of opinion about the behavior of Christians, and, frankly, we don't know if they got it right or not. I'm assuming they did because of what they did do right. They looked to Scripture, reason, and prayer, and trusted the rest to God.

We've gone from 120 believers huddled together after Jesus' ascension to two billion Christians today. The early believers started off right by looking to God for his will in their decisions.

Reflect and Discuss

1. The early followers of Jesus had knowledge of prophecy that prepared them for the changes they were to experience. Do modern Christians have the same need for biblical wisdom?

2. Are there big decisions you are making that can be informed by following the early believers' example?

3. Peter was not prohibited from service even after his denial of Jesus. Are there situations in the church today where forgiveness is needed in order to move forward to serve God?

CHAPTER 3

WELCOMING THE SPIRIT

(ACTS 2:1-13)

The Day of Pentecost changed everything for the followers of Jesus—and for us.

The band of 120 Jesus loyalists was still together that morning, engaged in the ten-day prayer meeting in the large upstairs room of a Jerusalem mansion. They stuck together, certain that Jesus would keep his word and send them the promised gift, the Holy Spirit. There were questions and uncertainty, an air of expectation, and maybe even frayed nerves in that room, but the people continued their watch—waiting and trusting.

It was Pentecost, one of three required Jewish holidays. Every male Jew living within twenty miles was legally required to come to Jerusalem, but thousands more traveled there from all over the ancient world. They were called the Diaspora, referring to the way they were dispersed in cities and provinces across the Roman Empire.

"Suddenly a sound like the blowing of a violent wind came from heaven and filled the whole house where they were sitting" (2:2). It sounded like a hurricane or a tornado and it drowned out the sound of their prayers and their shouts to one another. "What's happening?" "This is it!" A glance outdoors would have told them that this was no storm moving through the city. It was something supernatural that filled the whole house. From the description we can tell that it was not a wind, but *like* a wind: powerful and irresistible. "They saw what seemed to be tongues of fire that separated and came to rest on each of them" (2:3).

It was as if the ceiling was lapped in flames by a giant fiery tongue that split into 120 separate flames and came to settle on each one of them. Again, it wasn't actual fire or actual tongues, but those are the images that Luke chose to describe what was seen. No mention is made of fear or people running from the room. This wasn't terrifying or painful but exhilarating. After ten days of waiting, the people were caught in the middle of a miracle and in the supernatural presence of God himself, just like when Moses met God on Mount Sinai. "All of them were filled with the Holy Spirit and began to speak in other tongues as the Spirit enabled them" (2:4).

> Pentecost *means "fiftieth."* *(Compare the word to* Pentagon, *the Department of Defense headquarters in Washington, a building with five sides.) Pentecost was and is an annual Jewish holiday that comes fifty days after the Jewish holiday of Passover. It had a double historic significance: Pentecost commemorated the day when Moses met God on Mount Sinai to receive the Ten Commandments, which was believed to be fifty days after the nation of Israel left Egypt. God talked to Moses and there was thunder, lightning, and smoke.[1]*
>
> *Pentecost was the Jewish "Thanksgiving Day." It marked the end of the harvest and was sometimes called the Feast of Harvest or the Feast of Weeks because the harvest began at Passover and lasted 50 days—"a week of weeks" (seven weeks times seven days plus one). Because the weather was better at Pentecost in June than at Passover in April, it was easier to travel. Everyone got the day off.*

There were no words adequate to describe their experience. Their bodies and souls were saturated with the presence of God. That oneness and closeness filled them with warmth, fullness, awareness, and happiness beyond anything they had ever experienced. They were invigorated, empowered, and overwhelmed. And when they opened their mouths, out poured speech in foreign languages they had never learned. This was miraculous, like earlier supernatural events of water changed to wine in an instant, blindness cured with a touch, life returning to dead bodies.

Excitement filled them to bursting. They rushed out of their meeting room and into the streets of Jerusalem, to the marketplace and to the temple, where they encountered visitors to the city.

"Now there were staying in Jerusalem God-fearing Jews from every nation under heaven" (2:5). Luke didn't mean Chinese, Navajos, and Hawaiians. He was referring to the people and provinces in and around the Roman Empire where Jews then lived. Jesus' followers were speaking fluently in the languages of the five areas that made up what are now modern Turkey, Judea, Egypt, and the parts of Libya near Cyrene, North Africa. The witnesses—Romans, Cretans, and Arabs—were stunned that these Christians were talking to them in their native languages, particularly because most of the 120 were Jews from the northern province of Galilee. Around Jerusalem, Galileans were considered hicks, easily identified by their dress, manners, and accent. These were individuals unlikely to have mastered other languages. No wonder a crowd gathered; no wonder the onlookers were bewildered and captivated.

What they heard were Christ followers talking about the wonders of God. They spoke of Jesus, miracles, crucifixion, resurrection, the power of the Holy Spirit, forgiveness of sins, and eternal life. They expounded eloquently about what God had done for them and what God can do for others. The listeners were stunned. "Amazed and perplexed, they asked one another, 'What does this mean?' " (2:12).

These historic events were unprecedented and awe-inspiring, but some thought it was funny. They mocked the believers, proclaiming, "They have had too much wine."[2] Often, people who stand in the presence of God totally miss the Spirit.

But it was 9:00 a.m. They had been praying, not drinking. It was not spirits; it was the Spirit. In Acts 2:14-41, Peter took the

The Jesus Revolution

opportunity to address the crowd and delivered a passionate and persuasive sermon ending in this instruction: "Repent and be baptized, every one of you, in the name of Jesus Christ for the forgiveness of your sins. And you will receive the gift of the Holy Spirit. The promise is for you and your children, and for all who are far off—for all whom the Lord our God will call" (2:38-39).

And they did. The Bible says, "Those who accepted his message were baptized, and about three thousand were added to their number that day" (2:41).

But what did it mean? The Holy Spirit enabled those early believers to accomplish the impossible—to speak the good news of Jesus at a timely moment in history, when people of many nationalities were in Jerusalem. They, in turn, would be able to take the message home to their family, friends, and synagogues.

To us, this story shows that the Spirit is real, powerful, and supernatural. He does the unexpected. He is not controlled by us. He is the Spirit for people all over the world. The Holy Spirit fills us to empower us so that we can tell the wonders of God to others.

There was never another day like that Pentecost, never before and never again. It was a once-in-a-lifetime event. Although I want what they experienced—the wind to blow, the room to shake, the fire to fall, the Spirit to fill, and the miracles to happen—the Spirit doesn't do what I want. He does what he wants. He doesn't repeat Pentecost like a movie rerun. The Spirit is fresh and new every time. The sights and sounds of that amazing Pentecost were stunning, but the presence, power, excitement, and courage that he brings are available today. The Spirit of God is always powerful, always present, and always different. He is still full of surprises.

So, what do we do? We gather as they gathered. We pray as they prayed. We believe as they believed. We wait for and welcome the Holy Spirit. Subtle or spectacular, sooner or later, may the Holy Spirit fill us and do his great work within and through us.

16

Reflect and Discuss

1. Have you experienced "people who stand in the presence of God [but] totally miss the Spirit"?

2. The Holy Spirit is at work today. When have you witnessed his power?

3. Is the Holy Spirit a part of your day, every day? What changes can you make to be open to and aware of his presence?

CHAPTER 4

JOINING IN COMMUNITY

(ACTS 2:42-47)

After the high thrill of Pentecost, when three thousand new believers accepted the message of Jesus and were baptized, the followers and the new converts got together to do something characteristic of Christians. They formed a community of faith. The church of Jerusalem had grown exponentially, and now the believers continued their spiritual growth. A description in Acts 2:42-47 gives a detailed picture of the activities and characteristics of this group.

First, "they devoted themselves to the apostles' teaching" (2:42).

The church was based on the truth of God. The apostles' teaching refers to the doctrines of the Christian faith that the apostles had learned from Jesus and were still learning from the Holy Spirit. In other words, a church isn't a church just because a group of people get together and discuss religion. To be a Christian community means basing everything on the truth of God.

This was a learning church more than it was a teaching church.

The burden did not primarily rest on the apostles to teach but on the Christians to learn. Sometimes teachers are boring, disorganized, and inarticulate, and students learn despite the teachers' shortcomings. Sometimes teachers are brilliant and scintillating communicators but their students learn nothing. The best of

Christians learn because they are hungry for truth about God. The best churches are not dependent on the skills of their teachers. The Jerusalem church was far more than a first-century school, however. The people also dedicated themselves to fellowship. The word *fellowship* is a translation from *koinonia,* the Greek word for "common." In our vocabulary we call this "community." A community revolves around something shared: a neighborhood, business, political cause, medical issue, sport, hobby. With their shared faith in Jesus as Savior and Lord, the people of the Jerusalem church enjoyed fellowship with other believers that gave them warmth, security, and deep friendships.

They spent time together participating in "the breaking of bread." Certainly the group ate meals together, but this reference is to "*the* breaking of bread" indicating Christian communion. This is a meaningful spiritual discipline of remembering the sacrifices of Jesus through a symbolic ritual—eating bread to recall Jesus' body willingly given over to torture and death, and drinking wine to focus on his spilled blood. In those days communion was normally part of a regular meal rather than part of a church service as it often is today.

We're also told that they prayed. Prayer bonds Christians with God and with each other like nothing else. It is doubtful that there was a space big enough to hold the thousands in the Jerusalem church at one time, and it may not have been safe or expedient to gather that many Christians together anyway. More likely the people formed small groups. Prayer was not a new practice to people of Jewish descent. They were experienced through the generations in appealing to and conversing with God. However, they now had the Holy Spirit within them and they understood with gratitude that Jesus had died for them. Their prayers had new dimension. They prayed together and for each other.

The Christians celebrated the power of God that they saw and experienced firsthand. "Everyone was filled with awe, and many wonders and miraculous signs were done by the apostles" (2:43). It was exciting, exhilarating, overwhelming.

God is constantly at work, answering prayers and accomplishing wonders and miracles on earth. We hear reports of the touch of God in people's lives—healing from sickness and addictions, transforming lives, reconciling relationships. If we're not paying attention, we may begin to think of these stories as mere good news. When we're tuned into God and his power, we know that he is at work in our midst and we can't help but be awestruck.

Possessions stopped being "mine" and become "ours" as needed. "All the believers were together and had everything in common. Selling their possessions and goods, they gave to anyone as he had need" (2:44-45). This was not a practice ordered by Jesus, nor is there any indication it was taught by the apostles. It was a spontaneous, Spirit-driven desire to care for each other. Note that the believers continued to break bread in their homes and eat together, so not all homes were sold (2:46). This wasn't a commune or a strictly enforced activity that was practiced across the board. In other words, this was a description of the early church, not a prescription. Acts 2 records and describes what the Christians did but does not prescribe and require that all Christians everywhere sell their possessions. They were like Jesus. When there was a need, he went out of his way to give everything he had to help. These Christians were caring and compassionate toward those in need. Their eyes were open to the needs around them and they were willing to sacrifice to help. To lack compassion and action toward those who are needy is to lack loyalty to Jesus and his teaching.

The Jerusalem believers "broke bread in their homes and ate together" (2:46). In other words, they hung out together, socialized, and enjoyed one another's company. A gathering then wouldn't be much different than one now. There would have been jokes, laughter, stories, and deepening friendships. One dimension of their Christianity was pure enjoyment.

Worship was a vital part of this dynamic, young, and growing Jerusalem church. "Every day they continued to meet together in the temple courts" (2:46). Every day. When they weren't in the temple they were spending time in each other's homes, eating together "with glad and sincere hearts, praising God and enjoying the favor of all the people." God was central to life and central to the life of the community. Their joy and happiness was collective and contagious—so much so that outsiders were attracted.

It all sounds perfect. Could even this early community of believers, so close to Jesus' life on earth, have had difficulties and distractions? Were there people whom some of them didn't like or agree with, whose clothes didn't match, or whose facial expressions seemed insincere? From Luke's description of their community, it appears that they were full-time worshipers, action-oriented, and thoroughly connected with God. That probably didn't give them much time to be caught up with gossip, jealousy, or other negative activity. They were busy establishing a new church. Did they have differences and disputes? Were there some who were critical, dysfunctional, and cynical? I'm sure there were. But the heart-warming report in these verses focuses not on their differences but on their supernatural relationships in Jesus their Lord. It was about God and not about them. It was the beginning of all God wanted the church of Jesus Christ to be and become.

This does not mean that life was easy for them. We already know that some of these Christians were so desperate and needy that they required miracles from God and money from their friends just to have the basics of food, clothing, and shelter. Later in Acts, Luke recorded stories of believers singled out for beatings, imprisonment, and execution.

But it is heartening to read how content they were, how joyful, how fulfilled, and how closely they were surrounded by friends. In the same way that misery and criticism are contagious, joy spreads. This church had epidemic joy and it resulted in growth as people were attracted to those who had something different. "The Lord added to their number daily those who were being saved" (2:47). He wasn't just adding bodies or numbers—he was adding believers. Evangelism was one of the main activities of these early Christians. Jesus said that his followers would be his witnesses. Persuading or inspiring others to believe was their job, but they knew that actual salvation was an act of God. The Holy Spirit drew unbelievers to faith. "The Lord added to their number daily those who were being saved."

We cannot truly imagine the excitement and adrenaline that ran through those first church members. Many of them had known Jesus personally and remembered the sound of his voice. But their proximity and our historical distance in no way separates us from the opportunity to experience community in the way that Jesus intended. In our faith community we understand what it is like to be loved by people who are forgiving and who want the best for us. We experience the joy of serving others sacrificially. We worship and pray. We learn, not dependent on rousing teaching but on our own curiosity and desire to learn more about the Lord we love and want to serve. We live in our own time and know what it is to be part of a community of glad and sincere hearts.

Reflect and Discuss

1. What images does the word *fellowship* evoke for you?

2. Does the early believers' practice of fellowship change your view of fellowship?

3. How can you experience or initiate fellowship with someone who would not typically be your friend?

CHAPTER 5

GRASPING SALVATION

(ACTS 3:1-26)

The temple in Jerusalem was a wonder of the ancient world, the dazzling result of two generations' labor and King Herod's fortune. Positioned high on Mount Zion, with its gleaming, white marble and sparkling silver and gold accents, it was a structure built to impress. Elaborate porticoes—Solomon's Colonnade—surrounded the exterior of the temple. The walkway was named after an earlier king of Israel, the builder of the first temple, which was destroyed several centuries before. The outer perimeter of the colonnade was open to Gentiles as well as Jews and became a popular gathering place. Jesus had gone there often—usually to teach but at least once to chase away the merchants who multiplied until they crowded out the worshipers. The Colonnade was loud and busy with conversations, teaching, animals, people, praying, debating—and begging.

Acts 3 opens with Peter and John heading to the 3:00 p.m. prayer time at the temple. This was nothing unusual. Following each of the three daily sacrifices, there were prayer meetings, and religious people came like baseball fans to the home opener.

The temple was a prime gathering spot for beggars too, as all Jews were encouraged to give alms to the poor. Picture the chaotic and cacophonous scene the apostles entered. Have you ever walked into a crowd of beggars? If you've visited a Third World country, you probably have. Frankly, it's hard to know whom to help. There is a sense that if you put money into the hand of one, you'll be trampled by the rest. Yet how can anyone be so hardened as not to help the poorest of the poor?

That day there was a forty-something man in the sea of beggars, a senior citizen by first-century demographics (4:22). Born a paraplegic, he needed to be carried to his spot at the temple each day to ask for a few coins for his survival. Years of experience had taught him that his space by the Beautiful Gate, with its seventy-five-foot arch and wooden doors covered with expensive Corinthian brass, was the place to be. Getting a good spot was important because he couldn't move with the crowd.

It's hard to say what about him attracted the attention of Peter and John; there were many others vying for their attention. Just as they were about to enter the temple, the beggar called out his urgent request for money.

Peter stopped and "looked straight at him, as did John" (3:4). This must have been startling. People didn't usually meet his eye when they contributed their small sums to him—rich people didn't want to get that close to the poor and disabled—and the man didn't usually make eye contact with them, either. He knew that he was expected to look down in humility, not up in bold confidence. Besides, he couldn't linger long on any one passerby if he was going to target a thousand a day. This man not only held his gaze but also called back to him, "Look at us!" In hopes of snagging a bigger-than-usual contribution, the man obeyed.

Peter said: "In the name of Jesus Christ of Nazareth, walk" (3:6). Name *referred to everything about the person—all characteristics, personhood, words, deeds, power and authority. It was comprehensive. Peter went on to list a few of the attributes of Jesus: the "Holy and Righteous One" (3:14), the "author of life" (3:15), the one who suffered on the cross (3:18), the one raised from the dead (3:15), the one in heaven who promises to return (3:21), the one predicted by Moses (3:22-23), the one prophesied by every prophet from Samuel on down (3:24), the one promised to Abraham (3:25).*

Peter held out empty hands and made a non-cash offer: "Silver or gold I do not have, but what I have I give you. In the name of Jesus Christ of Nazareth, walk" (3:6).

The unnamed man must have been totally caught by surprise—disappointed that he wasn't going to get the money he wanted and flabbergasted by the proposed miracle. Who knows what went through his mind? Did he at that instant think, "Impossible!" or did his hopes rise? The possibility of healing was more than he could have dreamed of, an answer to his lifelong prayer. Before he had a chance to ask a question or turn to the next passerby for cash, Peter grasped his right hand and pulled him up.

For the first time in his life of more than four decades, the poor man stood eye-to-eye with other men. Feet that never felt full weight were firm on the ground. Ankles that never balanced a body became strong. With a helping hand from Peter, the man took his first steps. And then he ran, jumped, and shouted praises to God. I'm certain that Peter and John watched this with smiles of enjoyment. The man had only asked for money and Peter responded by giving him the freedom to walk—in the name of Jesus of Nazareth.

The ruckus drew attention and a crowd. People recognized the man immediately as the beggar, transformed. "They were filled with wonder and amazement at what had happened to him" (3:10).

The man quit jumping, latched onto Peter and John, and wouldn't let go. The historian Luke uses a term suggesting a police arrest to describe the way he held onto them. Even those just showing up had no doubt that a miracle had just occurred and Peter and John looked like the miracle workers.

Peter heard what the growing crowd was saying and knew what they were thinking. He asked, "Men of Israel, why does this surprise you? Why do you stare at us as if by our own power or godliness we had made this man walk?" (3:12). Now that he had their attention, he felt a sermon coming on—a good news sermon that started with the bad news.

The God of Abraham, Isaac and Jacob, the God of our fathers, has glorified his servant Jesus. You handed him over to be killed, and you disowned him before Pilate, though he had decided to let him go. You disowned the Holy and Righteous One and asked that a murderer be released to you. You killed the author of life. (3:13-15)

These were strong—some might say harsh—words. Just in case his listeners were inclined to wiggle out of their involvement, Peter reminded them that even after the Roman governor Pilate declared Jesus innocent, they still demanded his execution. Perhaps remembering his own triple denial of Jesus that same week, Peter cut them some slack: "Now, brothers, I know that you acted in ignorance, as did your leaders" (3:17). It was true; they didn't fully realize what they were doing, but they had participated in the shedding of innocent blood.

Then Peter threw them a lifeline: "Repent, then, and turn to God, so that your sins may be wiped out, that times of refreshing may come from the Lord" (3:19).

What was he asking of them? To admit guilt? Partly. But true repentance is the changing of one's mind and behavior, not just the admission of sin. Peter invited them to see Jesus differently— not as someone to be hated and crucified but as someone to be loved and honored. Believing that Jesus was the Savior promised by God was their pathway to salvation from God.

To be saved from anything assumes escape from something terrible—drowning, fire, disaster, death—which is a perfect description of what it means to be saved by Jesus. Believers who confess their belief in God's Son and repent are naturally changed by that decision. They escape the consequences of sin. They live for eternity with God.

But if Jesus saves someone, it doesn't start some time in the future, when they die; it starts now. Peter promised his audience "times of refreshing," which is a wonderfully evocative description of a life started over. That's what happens when we commit our lives to Jesus. We're still us but we're refreshed by God—and changed.

Even if Christians just died and stayed dead without going to heaven, it would still be good news to follow Jesus in this life. We would get God's refreshment and blessing in our lives right now. Living for him affects our relationships, pursuits, plans, and everyday experiences. It enables us to face difficulty, to reach out to others, to view life through different eyes. But there is an indescribable reward: when we turn away from our sin and follow Jesus as Savior and Leader, we gain heaven too.

Put yourself in the story. Today be a beggar. Ask God for whatever it is you want. Is it healing? Wisdom? Success? Money? But, listen hard and hear that the answer to whatever you ask starts with Jesus. It's all about him.

Reflect and Discuss

1. Was the man's belief a prerequisite for his healing? What can we learn from the man who was healed at the temple?

2. In what ways does your faith in Jesus improve your life?

3. How would starting with Jesus change you?

CHAPTER 6

LETTING JESUS LEAD

(ACTS 4:18-22)

With their whole hearts, Peter and John believed Jerusalem's empty tomb would change the world. God had raised Jesus from the dead and they were so convinced of the singular meaning of this miracle that nothing kept them quiet. However, their convictions would get them into trouble.

After the healing of the man outside the temple and Peter's blunt sermon that ensued, the religious authorities were "greatly disturbed" (4:2). They had Peter and John arrested to be tried before the Sanhedrin, Israel's supreme court. The apostles were held in jail overnight and may have faced a much longer prison stay if the authorities hadn't rightly worried about their growing popularity in Jerusalem. They feared making them into populist martyrs.

The judges held a closed session and, with their decision made, summoned the apostles.

> Then they called them in again and commanded them not to speak or teach at all in the name of Jesus. But Peter and John replied, "Judge for yourselves whether it is right in God's sight to obey you rather than God. For we cannot help speaking about what we have seen and heard."
>
> After further threats they let them go. They could not decide how to punish them, because all the people were praising

God for what had happened. For the man who was miraculously healed was over forty years old. (4:18-22)

What were the issues at the center of this controversy? God, through Peter and John, had healed the man who couldn't walk. One would presume this to be a good thing, but some had a different way of looking at it. To understand the thinking of the day, consider the time when Jesus was visiting Jerusalem and met a man born blind. Those around him asked a theological question: "Rabbi, who sinned, this man or his parents, that he was born blind?" (John 9:2). Jesus surprised them with his answer: " 'Neither this man nor his parents sinned,' said Jesus, 'but this happened so that the work of God might be displayed in his life' " (John 9:3). The original question highlighted the popular tendency to blame victims for their problems. If God punished someone, the reasoning went, it might be considered morally wrong to help that person escape his misery. Most of us know that such thinking is cold and unbiblical, although it may be more common in our generation than we imagine. When people are sick, poor, alienated, or desperate, others frequently blame them for their problems or at least take a hands-off approach. "That's their problem, not mine."

Peter and John's actions made clear that followers of Jesus were people of compassion, not judgment. Just like Jesus, they helped those in need. Their Teacher had demonstrated that even in cases where someone's behavior contributed to their desperate situation, one should reach out in kindness. Jesus' counterintuitive response to difficulty was one reason he drew crowds of thousands, and it explains why the early church converted an empire and changed the world.

Then there was the issue of the relationship of God to government—specifically, civil disobedience. The Sanhedrin ordered Peter and John "not to speak or teach at all in the name of Jesus." This was a directive with the authority of law forcefully behind it: "Comply or expect future charges and arrest." Having received these compelling instructions from the officials, Peter and John immediately and specifically replied that they would disobey the law. "Judge for yourselves whether it is right in God's sight to obey you rather than God. For we cannot help speaking about what we have seen and heard" (4:19-20). They let Jesus—not the laws of the land—lead them. The law was contrary to their instructions from Jesus and, therefore, could not bind them. Their higher allegiance was to him who had instructed them to "be my witnesses in Jerusalem, and in all Judea and Samaria, and to the ends of the earth" (Acts 1:8).

Doesn't the Bible clearly teach that Christians are to keep all laws? Christians were instructed to pay taxes to the oppressive and corrupt Roman government and even to submit to the immoral system of human slavery. "Submit yourselves for the Lord's sake to every authority instituted among men: whether to the king, as the supreme authority, or to governors, who are sent by him to punish those who do wrong and to commend those who do right" (1 Peter 2:13-14).

That seems clear—until we realize that the words were written by Peter, the same man quoted in Acts 4:20 promising to defy the orders to keep quiet about Jesus.

Life's most important decisions are seldom simple. The broad Christian principle here is that Jesus' followers are called to tell others the good news. Jesus died, rose again, and paid the price for sin. Eternal life is the reward for believers. Peter and John were prepared to become criminals in the eyes of others to carry this message into the world. It wasn't for their advantage but for the benefit and blessing of others.

They set a precedent. In coming years, they—and many other Christians—would be forced to choose Jesus over the laws of the government, sometimes with horrific consequences.

Several years ago, I traveled with three others to a Communist country where widespread persecution of Christians was sanctioned. The night before our flight, we stayed at a hotel in a nearby country and had dinner with a Christian leader who worked with the underground church. He told us amazing stories of persecution, evangelism, and modern miracles. Suddenly, he asked if we would take some literature with us on our flight the next day. I answered immediately, "No." I explained that it is against the law to smuggle literature into that country and I didn't want to break the law (I don't think that I mentioned not wanting to go to jail but that may have been my primary motivation). He did not take no as an answer. He said that he would have someone deliver some Bibles and other literature to our hotel early the next morning and we should ask God what we should do. "Definitely no," I said again.

Overnight, I made a decision. A Bible or two might be risky, but not impossible. However, I wasn't prepared for the following morning's delivery. It was a small library of Bibles, books about Christianity, study tools, and videos.

I truly can't explain why we did what we did. We divided up the Bibles, books, and videos among the four of us and loaded up every available space in our suitcases, carry-on bags, and purses. It was not a comfortable experience. When nearing our destination, the flight attendants distributed customs forms requesting our names, passport numbers, and the answers to pointed questions. Were we bringing guns, narcotics, or literature into the country? The four of us sat paralyzed over what to write. If we said we were not bringing literature, we were lying. If we checked that we were bringing books and Bibles, we were in serious trouble. ("Why yes, we just happen to have thousands of pages of literature in a language none of us can read!")

It was one of those moments when the Holy Spirit gave a simple solution that we would not have thought about ourselves. We didn't answer the question. We left it blank. I can't say that we were confident in our choice, but that's what we did. As we passed through immigration surrounded by armed guards and immigration officials, our forms were carefully scrutinized and all four of us were waved through.

What I next remember is the secret night meeting when we turned over the Bibles and literature to Christians from the underground church. Their faces will remain with me all my life.

You may want to criticize my lack of courage or condemn my actions as dishonest. For me, I was suddenly in the sandals of Peter and John who said, "Judge for yourselves whether it is right in God's sight to obey you rather than God. For we cannot help speaking about what we have seen and heard."

When facing prison or persecution, continue to exercise compassion and kindness. Let Jesus lead, "for we cannot help speaking about what we have seen and heard."

Reflect and Discuss

1. Imagine a modern-day situation in which some might blame the sufferer and avoid showing compassion. How can Christians make a difference?

2. How can we allow Jesus to lead even in risky circumstances?

3. As a Jesus follower, what does this phrase mean to you? "Life's most important decisions are seldom simple."

CHAPTER 7

PRAYING THROUGH THE PROBLEMS

(ACTS 4:23-31)

Released from prison and walking back through the streets of Jerusalem, John and Peter realized they were in trouble. Although they were free for the moment, the stern warning from the authorities to cease and desist their teaching was a tangible threat over their heads. They were now on a watch list and would not be traveling incognito. They might have felt a bit singled out. They had been following Jesus' instructions to the letter and it constantly landed them in trouble.

We all face more difficulty in life than we hope for or feel prepared to handle. Relationships are complicated and painful. Money concerns are intense. Friends betray us. Health issues come out of nowhere to consume us with pain and fear. Some problems are completely beyond our control and resources. The question is, "Where do you go when your problem is huge?"

Peter and John showed the way: "On their release, Peter and John went back to their own people and reported all that the chief priests and elders had said to them" (4:23). They knew exactly where to run, to the community of Christians they knew intimately—to people who would understand, stand by them, and pray for them. Note the phrase "went back." The relationships were firmly established before the crisis arrived.

I've spent a lifetime watching people in crisis. It is a difficult part of a pastor's ministry work, being present when terrible things happen to good people. Time and again I've observed that individuals who have Christian friends, are connected to the church, and have a team of mature believers who will pray for them do far better than those who don't. The time when you lose your job, receive a diagnosis of cancer, suffer the death of a family member, or face a natural disaster is not the best moment to start shopping around for someone who will pray for you.

Consider an uncomfortable thought: if you get slammed this week with the biggest problem of your life so far, who will pray for you? Who are your godly friends? Who will understand? Who will pray earnestly and consistently on your behalf? Blessed are those who have praying Christian friends.

When asked to pray, the friends of Peter and John knew precisely what to do. The praying had started in earnest before the arrival of the Holy Spirit, and their prayer lives had only deepened. They were experienced veterans of prayer.

Luke records that after they heard what had happened to Peter and John "they raised their voices together in prayer to God." I like the oneness and solidarity suggested by the word *together*. Did one person speak? Did they take turns? However the praying occurred, they were in it together.

"Sovereign Lord, ... you made the heaven and the earth and the sea, and everything in them. You spoke by the Holy Spirit through the mouth of your servant, our father David" (4:24-25). Their prayer begins with a humble acknowledgement of God's magnificence rather than a litany of requests. They knew him well.

> "You spoke by the Holy Spirit through the mouth of your servant, our father David:
> " 'Why do the nations rage
>   and the peoples plot in vain?
> The kings of the earth take their stand

and the rulers gather together
against the Lord
and against his Anointed One'
Indeed Herod and Pontius Pilate met together with the Gentiles
and the people of Israel in this city to conspire against your
holy servant Jesus, whom you anointed. They did what your
power and will had decided beforehand should happen."
(4:25-28)

Their prayer was an acknowledgment that God was behind the
events of history and even turned the nightmarish crucifixion of
Jesus into something good. He used the actions of Herod and
Pilate to accomplish human salvation through Jesus' death on the
cross. If he could do that, he could handle Peter and John's persecution. Their own words bolstered their faith: he had done it
before and could do it again.

Then they asked, "Now, Lord, consider their threats and enable
your servants to speak your word with great boldness. Stretch out
your hand to heal and perform miraculous signs and wonders
through the name of your holy servant Jesus" (4:29-30).

It is striking that the believers didn't pray for the problem to
evaporate. I would have been inclined to ask God to zap the
Sanhedrin or at least exempt the Christians from further persecution. But, instead of asking to be excused from difficulty, they
requested the ability to speak boldly despite the intimidation.
They prayed for God to perform healing and other miracles. They
wanted to show God's powers and to perform persuasive acts of
compassion and kindness. They were not vindictive. They didn't
seek retribution. They prayed for God to spectacularly triumph
over opposition with expressions of love.

Jesus had taught this principle—praying for our enemies. This
passage shows how closely aligned the believers had become
with him.

Like those Christians, start your prayers by acknowledging
God's sovereignty, not by asking for favors. This is just common
sense. Imagine yourself barging into the headquarters of a powerful world leader, marching down the carpeted aisle right up to the

desk and, without a word of greeting, demanding an array of goods and services. You wouldn't stalk into your boss's office and say, "Give me more money!" You'd begin with thoughtful and genuine dialogue. In the same way, remember with respect who God is and what he has already done for you. Ask for the gift of strength more than an instant solution to your issue. It isn't wrong to ask for the problem to be lifted, but it is much more important to realize and request that God enable us to face difficulties with faith.

Peter and John picked the right people to pray—people aligned with the will of God so the results were quick and powerful. "After they prayed, the place where they were meeting was shaken. And they were all filled with the Holy Spirit and spoke the word of God boldly" (4:31). Was it an earthquake, a supernatural event caused by the Spirit, or just a descriptive way of communicating the presence and power of God? We don't know for certain, but it is apparent something extraordinary again happened.

They were filled to the brim with the Holy Spirit. With supernatural joy and intense purpose, they were able to speak the message of Jesus boldly, exuding courage, confidence, and hope. It was the answer to prayers granted.

Would a movement of confidence and boldness have been possible without their fervent prayers? I think it's doubtful. Picture yourself in the same time period and circumstances. Your leaders have been threatened, you've seen your Teacher tortured to death. Would that put you in the frame of mind to witness? To preach on the street corners? To share freely with others the joy of the Christian life? No, something otherworldly happened, something the Holy Spirit orchestrated, organized, and implemented.

It was a great day at the house in Jerusalem, which—before the crucifixion and resurrection—had been just a pleasant home where people came for dinner now and again. Now it was an unofficial headquarters where the work of God was accomplished. The day began with a problem that looked insurmountable, and it brought people together. The Christians turned solemnly and trustingly to prayer and were not surprised by God's immediate and forceful response. The results were spectacular. But the problem didn't go away. In fact, this group would soon see their security deteriorate and their lives threatened.

This raises questions for me. When Christians face crushing problems, what are we supposed to do? Do we ask God for a miracle to fix the matter? Can God really heal Stage 4 cancer? Can God actually reconcile a marriage when one partner has broken trust through infidelity? Can God truly turn the outcome of an election or a war? Because, if he can, why doesn't he? If he can't, what's the point in believing in God?

Acts 4:24 reminds us that God is sovereign. He created the world, revealed himself to humans in the Bible, and is the God of history. He can do anything, but he created an ordered universe with laws of science that were his idea. Miracles are exceptions, not the norm. We pray for miracles and sometimes God says yes; sometimes he says no. But God is always the sovereign boss, and we trust him to give the right answer whether we like that answer or not. When God chooses to perform a miracle and solve our problem, we are deeply grateful. When God says no, we must be faithful and pray that he will give us the strength to make it through, make him look good, and be bold in our words for Jesus.

The great lesson from the prayer meeting is that God does not guarantee to make all our problems disappear. What God does is turn our human problems into supernatural victory through Jesus Christ.

Reflect and Discuss

1. Where and how might the early believers have developed their habits of prayer?

2. In order to enter God's presence with humility and respect, what words or actions could you use before making requests?

3. What would be the benefits of frequent and fervent prayer in your own life?

CHAPTER 8

LOOSENING HOLD OF POSSESSIONS

(ACTS 4:32-37)

Have you ever been so desperately poor you couldn't afford food for your next meal? Have you ever been wealthy enough to buy and store more food than you could possibly eat in a week? Either way, the story in Acts 4:32-37 is for you. It is the touching description of how the believers cared for one another as God's church was just getting started.

> All the believers were one in heart and mind. No one claimed that any of his possessions was his own, but they shared everything they had. With great power the apostles continued to testify to the resurrection of the Lord Jesus, and much grace was upon them all. There were no needy persons among them. For from time to time those who owned lands or houses sold them, brought the money from the sales and put it at the apostles' feet, and it was distributed to anyone as he had need. (4:32-35)

This is one of the most fascinating, encouraging, exciting, and sometimes controversial passages in the Bible. God performed a miracle in the church among the Christians. This supernatural event involved personal possessions, or, rather, how attached people were to them.

First, understand that people in first-century Jerusalem were as attracted to human comfort as we are today. They enjoyed pleasant homes, high-quality furniture, fine clothing, jewelry, and sturdy footwear. They looked forward to delicious meals. They had access to a bustling marketplace where traders from other countries brought dazzling riches, cloth, and food to sell. They were like people throughout history who have appreciated and enjoyed nice belongings, whether they could afford all they wanted or not. They were like us.

So the scenario described in Acts 4 is something to stop us in our tracks in wonder. It's about the human desire for comfort supplanted by the godly desire to share.

Luke's description of the group at this point in their history is touching: "All the believers were one in heart and mind." This phrase is uplifting because it shows that people *can* get along despite their differences. I grow weary of people fighting and arguing about everything. This group had worked out a better way, but their relationship was based on more than congeniality. It was unity. In some way that can't truly be explained, their hearts beat together. This doesn't mean that they were identical in personality and interests, which would be unnatural and, frankly, creepy. But they did agree on the important issues. That's as good as it gets.

"No one claimed that any of his possessions was his own, but they shared everything they had." It's disconcerting to read such a statement in twenty-first-century America where what's mine is mine and what's yours is yours. I may lend you my old canoe if you're a friend, but the notion that my belongings—furniture, clothing, cars—are up for grabs at any time makes me wince. If I have to relinquish my possessions and control of my stuff to have unity of heart and mind, I think I'll skip it. Confronted with this radical principle, I am forced to examine my priorities and beliefs. Am I so materialistic that possessions are more valuable to me than people? Do I love my house more than the community of Christians? Has my expectation that I am entitled to pursuit of personal possessions or financial security derailed my concern for the needs of my fellow believers?

Something had transformed these people. The Jerusalem believers were on a spiritual high after a supernatural encounter with God himself. Maybe you've had such an experience. God was there. You felt like he reached out and touched you. You felt his actual presence. You heard him. There are no words to tell someone else what it was like. You may even be afraid to talk about it because others would not understand the ecstasy. You were filled with awe, peace, warmth, and excitement at the same instant. That's what it was like for these believers. God turned the spiritual ecstasy into practical reality.

The Jerusalem Christians sold land and houses so they could help believers who needed money. This wasn't to construct church buildings or even to support missionaries. It was about making certain that everyone was cared for.

But this wasn't their only mission. "With great power the apostles continued to testify to the resurrection of the Lord Jesus, and much grace was upon them all" (4:33). There were social needs and spiritual needs and they met them both at the same time in the name of Jesus.

One without the other is incomplete. The first-century church did both. Like Jesus, they cared about the body and the soul. This is a fulfillment of God's dream for Israel recorded in Deuteronomy 15:4: "There should be no poor among you, for in the land the LORD your God is giving you to possess as your inheritance, he will richly bless you." The Christians responded as need arose: "From time to time those who owned lands or houses sold them." We don't learn the details—were they extra lots and second houses? The miracle wasn't that they sold and gave. The miracle was that they didn't wrap their arms around their possessions and say, "Mine." They shared with willing hearts—unselfishly, generously, and compassionately.

Would you be open to selling a possession to help someone who was hungry, jobless, or homeless? Would you be willing to donate money without getting a tax deduction? Would you be willing to turn the cash over to the apostles and let them decide who gets how much?

How much do you think you would be willing to give? I recently heard someone ask a thought-provoking question: *How much money would God have to give you in order for you to give away $100,000?* I had never really thought of it that way before. If God blessed you with an extra $200,000 would you give $100,000? Maybe it would take $1,000,000? Some people might need $10,000,000 before they would give away $100,000. Apparently the Jerusalem Christians thought that God had generously blessed them and they wanted to generously bless others.

The last two verses of Acts 4 contain a beautiful story of faith in action about a man named Joseph. He was a Levite from Cyprus and he had already earned the nickname Barnabas from the apostles. To them, he was "Son of Encouragement." He wasn't even a resident of Jerusalem—he was a visitor or tourist—but he was so united in heart and mind with the other Christians that he wanted to join in this financial sacrifice. He "sold a field he owned and brought the money and put it at the apostles' feet" (4:37). There must have been a need and he loved to help out. The amount he gave has been forgotten, but his generosity is remembered nearly two thousand years later.

The miracle was not about the money; it was Barnabas' changed outlook. Reading this passage we see how the Christians' hold on their money and belongings loosened—and we know that it was the direct result of the Holy Spirit sweeping through their lives. God does not divide our lives into separate departments with a wall between the spiritual and the practical. They are a seamless garment, inextricably woven together. When Jesus Christ is the Lord of life he is the Lord of all of life.

Rather than attributing this story to a different time, one that does not apply to us, we pray for the Spirit to change us. We pray that people will be more important to us than things. And then we expect beautiful, sacred transformation.

Reflect and Discuss

1. When it comes to sharing possessions, what impediments or struggles do you face? How can you overcome them?

2. Do you know anyone who impresses or inspires you with a generous attitude toward others?

3. What teachings in the Bible underscore the early believers' treatment of possessions?

CHAPTER 9

TELLING THE TRUTH TO GOD

(ACTS 5:1-11)

W hen we hear stories of sinful behavior by Christians, we wonder what God is thinking. *How can he allow someone to get away with that?* we might ask. From pastors to priests to church leaders to parishioners, people get themselves into trouble and appear to get by without much disturbance to their lives.

It is disconcerting when a fellow believer is found to be a hypocrite and a liar. These occasions bring uncomfortable questions to mind: Can Christians lie to God and get away with it? Ignore the call of God and still live a happy life? Break marriage vows and get away with it? Pretend to be generous when they are greedy? Does God automatically forgive and forget? We want to know if there are consequences for claiming to be a disciple of Jesus when living like a disciple of the devil.

Hypocrites can be found in the church, and that's hardly news. Some of us are not what we claim to be. Even the early church had its high-profile fakes. You can be sure that the story told in Acts 5:1-11 about a couple named Ananias and Sapphira was big news in its day, gossiped about for years afterward. Luke made a point to record it so the story has survived for centuries and serves as a lesson even today.

It occurred during the glory days of the brand new church in Jerusalem. New converts were flocking to Jesus by the thousands. Miracles were performed every day. Expressions of Christian love and generosity were abundant. It was the best of times and it would have been easy for Luke to focus his writing on only the positive. However, he saw the value in including the dark side too. Luke painted the portrait of the Jerusalem church, warts and all.

"Now a man named Ananias, together with his wife Sapphira, also sold a piece of property" (5:1). Ananias and Sapphira looked like the perfect Christian couple, with names to match: Ananias, a Hebrew word that means "God is gracious," and Sapphira, an Aramaic word for "beautiful." They were recipients of God's generosity—rich enough to own land, probably extra land beyond their home estate.

These two people were caught up in the center of all that was occurring in the church. They had experienced the powerful activity of the Holy Spirit. They witnessed the movement of generosity sweeping across the community of believers. They went home and discussed what God was inviting them to do. My guess is that they talked, and prayed, and decided together to sell their land and give money to the church as an act of worship to God. So they came back to church and announced their plans. It was a bit like signing a pledge card to contribute the cash as soon as the land sale closed. These are the type of people every church needs and honors. Godly. Generous. Good-hearted. But something went awry. Behind the façade was a conspiracy of premeditated deceit.

Perhaps there was an explanation. Maybe they intended to turn it all over, but at the last minute decided to hold back a portion of the money. It was a conspiracy of three, although I doubt they recognized their partner in the deal when they came up with the plan. Satan was part of the plot, out to damage if not destroy their fledgling church. He started with persecution on the outside and that backfired to make the Christians stronger. So he sneaked into the minds of Ananias and Sapphira to trick them into a conspiracy of deceit. "With his wife's full knowledge he kept back part of the money for himself, but brought the rest and put it at the apostles' feet" (5:2).

On the day of the cash transfer, Ananias and Sapphira apparently didn't travel together. Rather than wait for his wife, Ananias laid the cash at the feet of the Apostle Peter. I can see the smile on his face and hear the sense of pride and satisfaction in his voice. He was expecting a pat on the back and praise. In his worst nightmares Ananias could not have anticipated what happened next.

> Then Peter said, "Ananias, how is it that Satan has so filled your heart that you have lied to the Holy Spirit and have kept for yourself some of the money you received for the land? Didn't it belong to you before it was sold? And after it was sold, wasn't the money at your disposal? What made you think of doing such a thing? You have not lied to men but to God." (5:3-4)

Peter made stern accusations that must have set Ananias' heart pounding. It wasn't as if Ananias was required to give anything at all. Peter was very clear that this land belonged to Ananias and he could have done whatever he wanted with the land or the money. He could have kept it all. The sin was not in retaining some of the cash; rather, it was in backing out of his promise to God, lying to the Holy Spirit, and tricking the other believers into believing he was doing something he was not.

Peter said it well when he asked Ananias, "What made you think of doing such a thing?" What was he thinking? Did he believe God didn't know? Did he think God didn't care? Did he think he was going to get away with this? Was he really that stupid?

There is no record of Ananias' reply. "When Ananias heard this, he fell down and died. And great fear seized all who heard what had happened. Then the young men came forward, wrapped up his body, and carried him out and buried him" (5:5-6). We can only speculate on the cause of his death—a heart attack from sheer shock and fear, a rapid strike from God, or both. Either way, this was a church offering that no one soon forgot. The ushers came in, picked up his body, and took it out for burial.[1]

Hours later Sapphira showed up. She had no idea her husband was dead. Seeing her enter the room, the other believers hushed. Sapphira felt a small thrill of excitement. People were impressed with their gift, more impressed than she had even anticipated. She had expected them to thank her, but they actually seemed breathless. My first pastoral instincts would have been to take her aside and gently break the news of her husband's sudden demise. Church leader Peter was not so sensitive. To the contrary, he was so outraged by their assault on the integrity of the church and the cause of Jesus that he responded more like a police detective than a church pastor.

> Peter asked her, "Tell me, is this the price you and Ananias got for the land?"
> "Yes," she said, "that is the price." (5:8)

She was caught. She admitted it, and Peter vented his outrage.

> Peter said to her, "How could you agree to test the Spirit of the Lord? Look! The feet of the men who buried your husband are at the door, and they will carry you out also."
> At that moment she fell down at his feet and died. Then the young men came in and, finding her dead, carried her out and buried her beside her husband. Great fear seized the whole church and all who heard about these events. (5:1-10)

The last line of this scary story is a masterpiece of understatement. Reading it strikes fear in my heart two thousand years later.

But let's be clear: God was making a point, not setting a precedent. He was sending a message that following Jesus is serious business. It is a life of joy, otherwordly peace, and unexpected exhilaration, but it is not to be taken lightly. Stating the commitment is not enough.

Because our commitment is to God, we live to honor him. Everything we say and do reflects on him. We dare not dishonor the Holy Spirit, Jesus Christ, or God the Father.

Yes, the story of Ananias and Sapphira scares me. Yet I am grateful for it because it reminds me of God's holiness and my own unworthiness. I don't want a faith that is trivial or that lacks integrity. Because we are serving God himself, I expect the highest standards. I want a Christian life that is deep, intense, spiritually fulfilling, and real. I want a church that is all Jesus wants it to be.

Reflect and Discuss

1. The story of Ananias and Sapphira is a dramatic example of believers trying to cheat God. How do modern Christians attempt to cheat him?

2. How do you reconcile this account with stories of Christians behaving badly today?

3. How can Christians live with integrity?

CHAPTER 10

ENDURING PERSECUTION

(ACTS 5:17-42)

A lmost from the beginning, persecution was part of the Christian experience. Nero, the Roman Emperor from AD 54–68, blamed Christians for burning Rome and had them imprisoned, thrown to wild animals, burned alive, crucified. Peter and Paul were martyred. Domitian, emperor from AD 81–96, persecuted Christians for refusing to worship him as divine. The Apostle John was exiled to Patmos. Emperor Marcus Aurelius (AD 161–180) refused to protect Christians from civil uprisings. Decius (AD 249–251) ordered thousands killed, including the Bishop of Rome, for not offering sacrifices to him as emperor. Diocletian (AD 284–305) tried to eliminate Christianity by ordering church buildings burned, Bibles confiscated, pastors tortured, and Christian civil servants stripped of citizenship. Those who refused to recant were executed.[1] Tertullian, a second-century North African church leader and historian, grimly noted: "Kill us, torture us, condemn us, grind us to dust.... The more you mow us down, the more we grow."[2]

But persecution should come as no surprise to those who follow Jesus Christ, for he warned, "If they persecuted me, they will persecute you also" (John 15:20). Jesus' followers were becoming more visible. The powers given to the apostles by the Holy Spirit were being used to heal the sick. And although people flocked to Jerusalem with their sick friends and family members, no one dared join the band of Christians. The political and religious strain was palpable—and intimidating. It couldn't go on forever. One day the tension broke through. "Then the high priest and all his associates, who were members of the party of the Sadducees, were filled with jealousy. They arrested the apostles and put them in the public jail" (5:17-18).

The Sanhedrin, "the full assembly of the elders of Israel," had clearly ordered Peter and John not to teach anymore about Jesus; but the apostles deliberately defied the order in an act of civil disobedience—not only Peter and John but the other ten as well. The religious leaders had them all arrested and thrown in jail to await trial the next morning.

> But during the night an angel of the Lord opened the doors of the jail and brought them out. "Go, stand in the temple courts," he said, "and tell the people the full message of this new life."
> At daybreak they entered the temple courts, as they had been told, and began to teach the people. (5:19-21)

The apostles must have been dazed. Of course they knew that miracles occurred—they had witnessed supernatural occurrences many times—but they weren't expecting a "get out of jail free" card from God. That's the thing about miracles. They are unexpected, so they are fresh and exciting every time. Released from their confinement, the apostles went straight back out to preach.

When the Sanhedrin convened the next morning, they sent for the apostles and found the cells locked but empty, the guards still at their post. Bewilderment rippled through the crowd. Sadducees, who dominated the Sanhedrin, had an official stance on miracles—they didn't occur. While everyone was absorbing the reality of empty prison cells, someone came in and announced that the men were back in the temple courts teaching! Imagine their outrage. The captain of the guard took officers to go retrieve them, but Luke notes that they did not use force for fear of agitating the crowds.

Having brought the apostles, they made them appear before the Sanhedrin to be questioned by the high priest. "We gave you strict orders not to teach in this name," he said. "Yet you have filled Jerusalem with your teaching and are determined to make us guilty of this man's blood."

Peter and the other apostles replied: "We must obey God rather than men! The God of our fathers raised Jesus from the dead—whom you had killed by hanging him on a tree. God exalted him to his own right hand as Prince and Savior that he might give repentance and forgiveness of sins to Israel. We are witnesses of these things, and so is the Holy Spirit, whom God has given to those who obey him." (Acts 5:27-32)

That's bold talk. Picture the men standing there, completely outnumbered, but with their shoulders back and their voices strong. Talk about outspoken. Peter had come a long way since the night he had vehemently denied even *knowing* Jesus.

This story answers important questions about Christians who are persecuted for Jesus' sake.

Where is God when Christians are persecuted? He is there. He answers on our behalf. God is creative and fresh, powerful and innovative. He may send an angel or a miracle. Whatever his response, he is always present and always involved in the lives of persecuted believers.

What should a Christian do when caught in the middle? The apostles were set free from jail but were still stuck in the center of the controversy. Their order from the authorities was to "keep quiet." Now it was the believers against the law. Maybe they had wavered, uncertain and frightened, during their jail time, realizing the danger they were in. But the angel brought reassurance and a new certainty of their purpose: "Go, stand in the temple courts . . . and tell the people the full message of this new life."

Christians have often been caught between the call of God and the expectations of government, religion, family, neighbors, teachers, or employers. What are they to do? This story clearly says, "Obey God." It is sobering to realize that although he requires our obedience, God doesn't exempt Christians from difficulty for following through. Civil disobedience carries consequences—sometimes serious consequences. The apostles obeyed God's command to "tell the people the full message of this new life" and let the government choose its retaliation. Even without angels giving us instructions, our directions are clear. When faced with choosing between the expectations of God and the expectations of others, our obligation is to God.

What do we say when questioned? Peter and the apostles used persecution as an opportunity to speak the gospel. It is stunning to read their response to their dire situation. It is direct and to the point.

When the Sanhedrin heard the apostles' confident answer, they were furious and wanted the men executed. Suddenly everything was out of their hands again. The apostles were excused as their fate was discussed. Again they found themselves powerless. I'm sure they were hoping another angel would show up, but none did.

What does a Christian do when the situation is out of our control? Trust and let God work through others. In this case, the answer came through an unexpected source—a rabbi who was part of the discussion of their fate. Gamaliel urged the Sanhedrin to back off and wait, appealing to their logic and comparing Jesus to past rebels whose causes were soon forgotten.

> "Men of Israel, consider carefully what you intend to do to these men. . . . In the present case I advise you: Leave these men alone! Let them go! For if their purpose or activity is of human origin, it will fail. But if it is from God, you will not be able to stop these men; you will only find yourselves fighting against God." (5:35, 38-39)

The apostles never could have convinced the Sanhedrin of their purpose, so God used a respected teacher of the law to save the leaders of the new Christian church.

The apostles paid a price. The Sanhedrin agreed to release the apostles, but only after a flogging—a whipping typically so severe that many prisoners died afterward from blood loss. It's what was done to Jesus before he was crucified.

How should a Christian handle suffering that comes with having faith in Jesus? The apostles showed the way. After the flogging they left "rejoicing because they had been counted worthy of suffering disgrace for the Name" (5:41).

Why would anyone rejoice in severe physical and psychological suffering? The apostles believed their "disgrace" was really an honor. Perhaps God reminded them of Jesus' teaching during one of his most famous sermons:

> "Blessed are those who are persecuted because of
>   righteousness,
> for theirs is the kingdom of heaven.
>   Blessed are you when people insult you, persecute you and falsely say all kinds of evil against you because of me. Rejoice and be glad, because great is your reward in heaven, for in the same way they persecuted the prophets who were before you."
> (Matthew 5:10-12)

Persecution of Christians was not limited to the Roman Empire two thousand years ago. It has, in fact, increased. There were more martyrs for Jesus Christ in the twentieth century than in all the previous nineteen centuries combined.[3] In the twenty-first century, there is persecution in Vietnam, North Korea, China, Sudan, and many other countries. While Christian commitment may be comfortable for many Americans, suffering for faith in Jesus is very real for thousands of people around the world.

An organization called FaithWorks lists ways that people of faith may experience bias and persecution and it is a frightening compilation: (1) Disapproval, (2) Ridicule, (3) Pressure to conform, (4) Loss of educational opportunities, (5) Economic sanctions, (6) Shunning, (7) Alienation from community, (8) Loss of employment, (9) Loss of property, (10) Physical abuse, (11) Mob violence, (12) Harassment by officials, (13) Kidnapping, (14) Forced labor, (15) Imprisonment, (16) Physical torture, and

(17) Murder or execution.[4] If you faced these kinds of persecution, how would you respond?

The Christians of Acts faced persecution and endured in their faith. They were willing to go anywhere, do anything, and suffer greatly for Jesus Christ their Lord. "They never stopped teaching and proclaiming the good news that Jesus is the Christ" (5:42).

Reflect and Discuss

1. What experiences prepared Peter and John for confrontation?

2. In what ways does the Holy Spirit protect and strengthen Christians suffering persecution?

3. How would severe persecution affect your faith?

ORGANIZING TO GROW

(ACTS 6:1-7)

The growth of the Jerusalem church was threatened when the apostles ran up against the strategies of the devil himself. This was nothing new—Satan had been creating conflict since the beginning of human history. According to the English scholar John R. W. Stott, those strategies continue today in persecution, corruption, and distraction.[1]

Everything had been going well. Thousands of people were becoming followers of Jesus and the church was booming. Maybe their guard was down. People started feeling strong and untouchable.

Then came persecution. Government and religious leaders arrested disciples of Jesus, threw them into jail, and flogged them mercilessly. But persecution had the opposite of its intended effect. It energized the Christians and made them even more zealous to spread the word. More believers were drawn in, and the church continued to grow.

Then came corruption. Two church members, Ananias and Sapphira, tried to cheat the church out of promised funds. These tactics threatened to poison the church from the inside. But Ananias and Sapphira were abruptly struck dead. End of controversy. Corruption ceased. Again, the church boomed and the Christians were filled with fear of the Lord, overflowing generosity, and a desire to share the news of Jesus.

> *Hebrew Jews made up the majority of Jews in Jerusalem. They were Aramaic-speaking and proudly traced their roots to ancient times. Greek Jews were the minority. Their ancestors had moved away from Palestine to other parts of the ancient world, where they had adopted Greek culture—language, clothes, and lifestyle. Although some had moved to Jerusalem, the native Judeans always considered them outsiders and foreigners. They spoke different languages, had different ways of thinking, and even worshiped in different synagogues. So imagine these two groups becoming Christians and worshiping together in the same Jerusalem church.*

Then came distraction. It started with a few gripers, complainers, critics, whiners, gossipers—you know the type—and it grew into a full-blown controversy.

The church had a practice of collecting food in the synagogues and distributing it each day to needy widows. A widow in those days was in a very precarious economic situation, with no means of earning money for life's necessities. The church leaders had developed a compassionate way to meet their needs.[2] "In those days when the number of disciples was increasing, the Grecian Jews among them complained against the Hebraic Jews because their widows were being overlooked in the daily distribution of food" (6:1).

The Greek Jews had a legitimate gripe, caused, perhaps, not by prejudice but by poor administration. Whatever the reason, they were in the minority and felt powerless. They went right to the top of the leadership organization, the twelve apostles. (Isn't that what we all like to do?)

> So the Twelve gathered all the disciples together and said, "It would not be right for us to neglect the ministry of the word of God in order to wait on tables. Brothers, choose seven men from among you who are known to be full of the Spirit and wisdom. We will turn this responsibility over to them and will give our attention to prayer and the ministry of the word." (6:2-4)

The apostles showed supernatural wisdom and brilliant leadership skills. They couldn't micromanage every problem for the approximately 15,000 people now part of the Jerusalem church. This had to be handled on a different level by other leaders. Becoming personally involved in hearing complaints and managing day-to-day operations wouldn't leave adequate time to teach the word of God and pray, which would leave the church spiritually anemic.

Their response was God-inspired. They chose seven who were all Greek Jews (Acts 6:5). These men spoke Greek, understood Greek culture, and were trusted by the Greek minority in the church. Everybody was happy. Their decision kept the church organized and poised for success and growth. They defeated the strategies of Satan to distract the church of Jesus Christ through conflict. Everyone was pleased. More important, "The word of God spread. The number of disciples in Jerusalem increased rapidly, and a large number of priests became obedient to the faith" (6:7). Instead of allowing the complaining to escalate into a crisis, they responded in a godly manner, using organizational skills to diffuse stress.

The church today faces similar danger of derailment, whether from small issues of disagreement that escalate or Christians who create controversy.

The Jerusalem church showed that it was willing to accomplish God's purposes in a fresh way to diffuse disagreement. It was open to new approaches, experimentation, and risks. Missionaries are doing this today in predominantly non-Christian countries. Many of the traditional approaches of missions have been ineffective and even counterproductive. New ventures encourage people to retain their culture while becoming followers of Jesus. They pray with hands open, gather on Fridays to pray, avoid drinking alcohol and eating pork—and believe in the Bible and Jesus. It's a new approach and it is growing the church for Jesus. Other missionaries are working among people through business ventures that give them the opportunity to share the gospel. It's a modern example of Christians who are full of the Spirit and wisdom.

Complainers are still in our midst. They don't think they're complainers—they believe they're wiser, more godly, and helpful. But they can contaminate others with their attitude. When an approach is self-righteous, know-it-all, and accusatory, it can draw in others and take the focus off Jesus. It can hinder the work of God.

Here's what the Bible says: "Do not grumble" (1 Corinthians 10:10). "Do everything without complaining or arguing" (Philippians 2:14). "The entire law is summed up in a single command: 'Love your neighbor as yourself.' If you keep on biting and devouring each other, watch out or you will be destroyed by each other" (Galatians 5:14-15).

Getting along with other people can be a challenge. Brothers and sisters fight. Husbands and wives argue. Business partners disagree. Ethnic groups all have their prejudices. Twenty-first-century churches are no exception. Christians can differ over culture, language, and even worship or music style differences. Like the Jerusalem church we can resolve differences, never forgetting that the church is a supernatural entity, the body of Christ.

The Jerusalem church demonstrated for us an amazing combination of spirituality and common sense. Prayer and teaching the word of God were top priorities. When an issue got in the way, the apostles wisely came up with a commonsense approach. They kept first things first.

Reflect and Discuss

1. Name ways that you have seen Satan's strategies—persecution, corruption, and distraction—in practice.

2. Is it realistic to believe Christians can overcome differences and retain their love for one another as fellow believers? Why or why not?

3. Getting along with other people can be a challenge, and disagreement among Christians is inevitable. What are effective ways to diffuse disagreement within the church?

CHAPTER 12

REMAINING FAITHFUL

(ACTS 6:8-15)

B ad things happen to innocent people.
Luke's writings in Acts include the tale of a wrongly
accused prisoner, Stephen, a Jew living in Jerusalem.
With his Greek name he probably belonged to the Diaspora—a
class of Jews who had been dispersed around the Roman world
and who had adopted the Greek language and culture. His name
means "crown," which hints that his parents had high expectations for him from the time he was born. He probably belonged to
one of the Greek synagogues in Jerusalem that catered to Jews
who had immigrated from outside Palestine. We don't know if he
was rich or poor, educated or ignorant, short or tall, handsome or
homely, married or single, young or old.

What we most know about Stephen is his character. From the
description we learn he was "a man full of God's grace and
power" who did "great wonders and miraculous signs among the
people" (6:8). Stephen was an amazingly godly, spiritual, and
wise follower of Jesus. Those who knew him considered him a
person of sterling character and integrity. He was chosen to take
care of the church's finances and widows. He was the kind of
friend you could trust with your money and your mother. Stephen
was a truly good man who came under severe attack. "Opposition
arose, however, from members of the Synagogue of the Freedmen

(as it was called)—Jews of Cyrene and Alexandria as well as the provinces of Cilicia and Asia" (6:9).

"The Synagogue of the Freedman" refers to people who were once slaves to the Romans but were set free. In 63 BC, the Roman General Pompey took thousands of Jews into slavery. Later most of them were freed and some migrated back to Jerusalem, where they established their own synagogue. The other opponents of Stephen were from Cyrene (modern Libya), Alexandria (Egypt), Cilicia, and Asia (Roman provinces in the area of modern Turkey). It sounds like each group had its own synagogue. They were all people like Stephen, from the Greek culture and part of the Jewish religious minority. In all probability at least some of them belonged to the same synagogue that Stephen had belonged to. The opposition was not from Romans, not from pagans, not from another race or religion. The opposition was from Stephen's friends, people just like him.

"These men began to argue with Stephen, but they could not stand up against his wisdom or the Spirit by whom he spoke" (6:9-10). At first they tried to argue with Stephen. He was a Jew who believed in Jesus as his Messiah sent from God. They disagreed and hoped to defeat Stephen in debate. It started as a theological dispute—a clash of ideas and beliefs. Stephen was smart and a good debater. Truth was on his side. The others were no match and quickly lost the upper hand in the disagreement.

When they couldn't win the argument, they switched to a more lethal approach. You're familiar with this tactic if you have seen political ads during American election years. One strategy is to start campaigning for support with appealing photographs of the candidate plus a presentation of policies and persuasive points in order to win on persona and platform. If that doesn't work, the next step is to attack. The opponents of Stephen started with debate. They lost the argument and started to attack this man of sterling character with lies and inflammatory statements.

> Then they secretly persuaded some men to say, "We have heard Stephen speak words of blasphemy against Moses and against God."

So they stirred up the people and the elders and the teachers of the law. (6:11-12)

It is very difficult to defend oneself against this kind of attack. Stephen never tried. There is not one word of an attempt to shield himself, answer his critics, or return the attack. He could have. Stephen was a miracle worker who performed "great wonders and miraculous signs among the people," but he chose not to use these supernatural powers for his own protection.

Imagine the hurt of having your friends turn against you. These were his people. They belonged to the same ethnic, religious, and social group. His friends had become his enemies.

They seized Stephen and brought him before the Sanhedrin. They produced false witnesses, who testified, "This fellow never stops speaking against this holy place and against the law. For we have heard him say that this Jesus of Nazareth will destroy this place and change the customs Moses handed down to us." (6:12-14)

The accusations leveled against Stephen were serious to first-century Jews. They accused him of blasphemy against Moses and God. They mentioned Jesus' teaching that he would destroy the temple. Jesus had said that the temple would be destroyed and raised back up in three days, but they skewed the context and meaning. He was referring to his body, not the literal temple building. Jesus taught that the law was completed in him as the Messiah; this wasn't disrespect for the Jewish law but a fulfillment. Stephen's critics twisted and distorted the teachings of Jesus in order to attack this honorable man.

There is an important lesson here for Christians. When reading books, newsletters, emails, blogs, and websites, beware of those who make personal attacks. When you listen to radio programs or watch television programs, look out for those who take truth and twist it to fit their purposes or to stir up anxiety and trouble. Be cautious of anyone who claims to be a Christian yet attacks other believers.

Stephen was in serious trouble. His accusers were well organized and willing to use any deceit to win. He was standing trial before the same Sanhedrin that had convicted and condemned Jesus and imprisoned and beaten Peter and the other apostles. It didn't look good. But God had not forgotten him.

"All who were sitting in the Sanhedrin looked intently at Stephen, and they saw that his face was like the face of an angel" (6:15). Stephen's face glowed with a supernatural radiance. They couldn't take their eyes off him. This same glow had come to Moses when he met with God and delivered the law to the Jewish people.

What are we to make of this? God made Stephen's face radiant but did not set him free from jail. In fact, after delivering an impassioned and spirit-filled message (7:2-53), Stephen was stoned to death by the same men whom he had once counted as his friends.

Stephen is an important teacher for twenty-first-century Christians too. He shows us in grim, realistic detail that we can be God-fearing people who do right and yet still get taken down by the bad guys. Being full of faith and the Holy Spirit doesn't mean that life is easy or your dreams come true. Good and godly Christians get fired from jobs and suffer terminal illness and broken relationships. We live in a sinful world where people around us—and we ourselves—play into the evil strategies of Satan.

Where does that leave us? As Christians we are commanded to do what is right no matter how the situation is likely to come out. Along the way we trust God for the ultimate outcome whether we live to see it or not.

This is not just the biography of a good man who got a bad deal. Luke includes the story of Stephen in Acts because he knew there was more to the story. The church went on to change the world and Stephen was part of that history. Although Stephen did not live to see the outcome, he was a part of it. God is still at war against sin and Satan. The battle is dangerous and there are casualties in the conflict. Stephen is one person who lived for Jesus when it was dangerous and even deadly. Stephen was faithful to

God and suffered as a result, and he died before he witnessed the difference his life made.

There are strong indications that one of Stephen's accusers was a Greek Jew from Cilicia who lived in Jerusalem. This man later admitted that he was there and part of the enemy crowd. During the following years he could not get Stephen out of his mind—the man of goodness and godliness whose unjust arrest, trial, and execution he had witnessed and approved. God used the witness of Stephen to draw him to Jesus. This man's name was Paul—an opponent of Stephen who became the apostle of God and the author of much of the New Testament.

As Christians we are called to be like Stephen. Regardless of the outcome, we are to remain faithful to God even when up against enemies, critics, setbacks, illness, injustice, prejudice, and every other kind of opposition. No matter what, be faithful to Jesus for Jesus' sake, not because everything turns out well but because it is right and a powerful witness.

Reflect and Discuss

1. Without Stephen, what changes would there be to the story of the early church?

2. "Being full of faith and the Holy Spirit doesn't mean that life is easy or your dreams come true." Do you find this a hard truth to live with?

3. What strategies do you use to remain faithful when you face obstacles?

CHAPTER 13

CONVERTING THE UNCONVERTIBLE

(ACTS 9:1-31)

H ave you ever been shocked by the spiritual conversion of someone you *never* expected to change? The Holy Spirit has touched people's hearts from the beginning, and no one had a more dramatic conversion to Christianity than Saul. It couldn't have happened to a more unlikely candidate, a man who took sadistic pleasure in tracking down Jesus' followers and having them cruelly prosecuted. But while he was "still breathing out murderous threats against the Lord's disciples" (9:1), he had an extremely close encounter with Jesus on the road to Damascus, where he intended to arrest followers of "the Way." The Bible says that "suddenly a light from heaven flashed around him. He fell to the ground and heard a voice say to him, 'Saul, Saul, why do you persecute me?'" (9:3-4). Jesus had Saul's attention.

"Who are you, Lord?" Saul asked.

"I am Jesus, whom you are persecuting," he replied. "Now get up and go into the city, and you will be told what you must do."

The men traveling with Saul stood there speechless; they heard the sound but did not see anyone. Saul got up from the ground, but when he opened his eyes he could see nothing. So they led him by the hand into Damascus. For three days he was blind, and did not eat or drink anything. (9:5-7)

Saul had an immediate change of heart and mind. It was as though that flash of light turned him into a different person. He spent several days with the disciples in Damascus—praying or reflecting or repenting—then went out to the synagogue, his sight restored and a passion for a new message burning in his heart. Because he had been an outspoken critic of Jesus' followers, the Jews he met there had no reason to distrust him. But as they gathered to listen, his teaching baffled them. He set out powerful and persuasive facts, giving evidence that Jesus was the Messiah sent from God. Saul didn't just preach; he laid out an empirical case for others to convert their beliefs!

It didn't take his audience long to figure out that Saul had switched sides. They conspired to murder him: "After many days had gone by, the Jews conspired to kill him, but Saul learned of their plan. Day and night they kept close watch on the city gates in order to kill him" (9:23-24).

Damascus, like many ancient cities, was protected by thick stone walls. The protective walls around cities were typically wide enough to drive multiple chariots side-by-side on the top. These massive barriers were built to keep enemies out. In Saul's case, they trapped him inside.

He was once the hunter and now he was the hunted. He was once the murderer and now the crowd was out to murder him. Who would he turn to for help? We must admire the faith and forgiveness of the believers who accepted Saul as a truly transformed man despite his ugly past. They came up with a daring plan to help him escape. From a home built atop the wall, these fellow believers secretly lowered him beyond the city wall with a basket and ropes.

The report in Acts 9 says that Saul went to Jerusalem, but to fill in the timeline we need to check out some other parts of the New Testament. Galatians 1:17-18 gives more detail: "I went immediately into Arabia and later returned to Damascus. Then after three years, I went up to Jerusalem."

An ancient map shows that back then the northwest corner of Arabia wasn't very far from Damascus. Saul escaped from Damascus into the desert, perhaps for as long as three years. Then he returned to Damascus and eventually to Jerusalem.

Why would God take Saul to the Arabian desert? Didn't God want Saul to become a great missionary to the Roman Empire? Why wait three years? God takes time to get us ready for what he calls us to do.

When I was a college student I wanted to quit school and go serve God somewhere. Going to college seemed like a waste of time. I wrote a letter to my father telling him my thoughts and received a return letter that I wish I had saved. My father wrote that when he was my age he wanted to do the same thing. He talked to his mentor, a Presbyterian minister named Donald Barnhouse, who told him if he had only ten years to serve God he would spend nine in preparation and one in service. He was convinced he would accomplish more in that one year than the person who spent one year in preparation and nine years in service.

Saul spent three years with God getting ready—sharpening the axe. Finally, he was ready to go back to Jerusalem. Was Saul accepted with open arms? Hardly. The believers in Jerusalem had been persecuted, arrested, and imprisoned by him and had no reason to trust him now. Likewise, the Jews who thought Jesus' disciples were heretics believed Saul was a traitor. It seems he could have gone almost anywhere else to get a fresh start. But he didn't. Acts 9:26-30 says:

> When [Saul] came to Jerusalem, he tried to join the disciples, but they were all afraid of him, not believing that he really was a disciple. But Barnabas took him and brought him to the apostles. He told them how Saul on his journey had seen the Lord and that the Lord had spoken to him, and how in Damascus he had preached fearlessly in the name of Jesus. So Saul stayed with them and moved about freely in Jerusalem, speaking boldly in the name of the Lord. He talked and debated with the

Grecian Jews, but they tried to kill him. When the brothers learned of this, they took him down to Caesarea and sent him off to Tarsus.

Once again, Barnabas came to the rescue. Barnabas introduced Saul to the church and vouched for him. Paul was soon accepted and became a formidable force for the faith in Jerusalem. With his Greek background and rabbinical training, he was a master at explaining that Jesus was the Messiah sent by God. But there were some religious Jews who were not persuaded. To the contrary, they were upset and angry because of what Saul taught—so they conspired to murder him. It seems that everywhere Saul went there were potential assassins.

The followers of Jesus who initially rejected him decided to protect him. The leaders of the church marched him from Jerusalem in the hills to the Mediterranean seaport of Caesarea and shipped him back to Tarsus where he was born. They recognized God's hand on Saul's life and didn't want to lose him to a murderer. Sometimes Christians need to stay and fight. Sometimes Christians need to cut and run. This time Paul needed to just get out of town until the controversy cooled down. Once Saul left Jerusalem, everyone breathed a little easier. "Then the church throughout Judea, Galilee and Samaria enjoyed a time of peace. It was strengthened; and encouraged by the Holy Spirit, it grew in numbers, living in the fear of the Lord" (9:31).

If God can change anti-Jesus, violent, angry, murderous Saul into a believer and a saint, then he can change *anyone*. A conversion may be dramatic like Paul's or as subtle as a breathed prayer. Sometimes complete change takes time. Saul was converted in a blazing light with Jesus talking out loud, but he needed three years in the desert to be changed into the man of God that Jesus wanted him to be.

The story of Saul is a beautiful reminder of the power of God. No matter a person's background and history, God can create a believer filled with the Holy Spirit. This is true for you and for the people in your life who seem beyond his reach. Don't give in to doubt. Never stop praying. And always have hope.

Reflect and Discuss

1. Why would God choose Saul for conversion at this point in the history of the church?

2. Can you think of other people—historical or contemporary—who have experienced dramatic conversions? Subtle conversions?

3. Is it difficult to have faith when praying for people in your life who have separated themselves from God? What scriptures give you hope?

CHAPTER 14

IMITATING JESUS

(ACTS 14:8-20)

Times were tough—even deeply discouraging. James, the brother of John, had been put to death "with the sword" (Acts 12:2). Peter, also, had been seized and thrown into prison until an angel sent by God rescued him. Followers of Jesus were not free to practice their faith. Despite these difficulties Luke wrote: "The word of God continued to increase and spread" (12:24).

Meanwhile, in the Antioch church, the Holy Spirit urged the believers to do something daring: "Set apart for me Barnabas and Saul for the work to which I have called them" (Acts 13:2). And they obeyed. "After they had fasted and prayed, they placed their hands on them and sent them off" (13:3). Saul (who came to be known as Paul) and Barnabas began a journey across the empire.

As the first traveling missionaries, Paul and Barnabas had intimate knowledge of the challenges ahead of them. They were about to come face-to-face with scorn, attack, and the disinterest of people who knew nothing about the Scriptures and its prophecies. They showed remarkable understanding of ways to speak to all kinds of people, not just those with whom they were most familiar. Were their tactics intuitive or Spirit-led? We don't know.

They had traveled across the Roman Empire going from synagogue to synagogue teaching religious Jews about Jesus and salvation from sin, referring to Scripture and prophecy as evidence for belief. But when they came to Lystra, a town that was part of the Roman empire (in what we now call the country of Turkey), there was no synagogue and no religious community. This audience knew nothing of the Bible or of God. When Paul talked about Jesus, there is no report of people responding as they had in other towns where unbelievers clamored to join the Christian movement.

Certainly these people were not surprised to hear a teacher lecturing on his beliefs. In those days traveling philosophers often stood on street corners and expounded on their beliefs. Crowds gathered to listen—especially if a stranger showed up with intriguing new ideas. Paul wasn't intimidated by the possibility of his Christian teachings competing in the marketplace with pagan ideas, convinced as he was that the gospel of Jesus Christ was more than a match for any belief system.

But in this scenario, Paul didn't limit his rhetoric to an intellectual or philosophic slant. He addressed human need as well. Paul looked over the crowd and his eyes fell on a man who had been born with a congenital anomaly of his feet. "In Lystra there sat a man crippled in his feet, who was lame from birth and had never walked. He listened to Paul as he was speaking" (14:8-9a). In those days any disability typically meant survival by begging and a lifetime of poverty. Faith and compassion compelled Paul to address the man and show him—and the gathered crowd—the power of God's love. "Paul looked directly at him, saw that he had faith to be healed and called out, 'Stand up on your feet!' At that, the man jumped up and began to walk" (14:9b-10).

Paul emulated Jesus by addressing the man's physical need for healing. Time after time, Jesus' miracles centered on the physical. He didn't put on supernatural shows to convince people that he was God's Son. He met their needs. He changed water to wine at a party. He healed sick children. He fed hungry mouths. He cured the people who were blind or had a physical disability. He raised the dead. And *then* he taught about God and eternal life. Paul followed Jesus' example and something totally unexpected happened. The crowd went wild. The witnesses started to worship Paul and Barnabas. They shouted, "The gods have come down to us in human form!" (14:11). They called Barnabas "Zeus" and Paul "Hermes."

There is a backstory that helps make sense of this strange reaction. The Roman poet Ovid wrote about an earlier incident occurring not far from Lystra. It was reported that two pagan gods disguised themselves as men and came to visit nearby— Zeus (the "top god," called "Jupiter" by the Romans) and Hermes (the son of Zeus, the official messenger of the gods, called "Mercury" by the Romans). These visiting deities, Ovid wrote, were treated poorly because no one recognized them as gods, and the locals suffered the consequences for alienating them. However, a couple named Philemon and Baucis welcomed them into their home. Zeus and Hermes richly rewarded this couple for their hospitality.[1]

So the crowds at Lystra saw the miracle and jumped to conclusions, assuming Paul and Barnabas were Zeus and Hermes on a second visit. They quickly decided to offer sacrifices to them. The people were speaking excitedly in their native dialect of Lycaonian so Paul and Barnabas didn't understand; they guessed that their audience was enthused about Jesus and they got caught up in the thrill of the moment until they realized with horror what was happening.

> The priest of Zeus, whose temple was just outside the city, brought bulls and wreaths to the city gates because he and the crowd wanted to offer sacrifices to them.
>
> But when the apostles Barnabas and Paul heard of this, they tore their clothes and rushed out into the crowd, shouting: "Men, why are you doing this? We too are only men, human like you." (14:13-15a)

Paul and Barnabas not only rejected the praise; they were outraged. They ripped their clothes in protest and insisted that they were ordinary men, refusing to become celebrities and instead glorifying God.

Paul's next words were a far contrast from the way he typically taught in the synagogues. When preaching to Jews he liked to quote the Hebrew Scriptures and pointed out the multitude of ways Jesus fulfilled prophecies made hundreds of years before his birth. But he knew this strategy wouldn't work in Lystra, where people knew nothing about the Scriptures and didn't care. So Paul looked for common ground. He talked about creation, nature, and the environment.

> "We are bringing you good news, telling you to turn from these worthless things to the living God, who made heaven and earth and sea and everything in them. In the past, he let all nations go their own way. Yet he has not left himself without testimony: He has shown kindness by giving you rain from heaven and crops in their seasons; he provides you with plenty of food and fills your hearts with joy." (14:15b-17)

What an interesting approach to evangelism. Paul didn't begin with Jesus, the Bible, repentance, or the cross. He began with God's natural creation, something of particular interest and enjoyment to his audience. His empathy and identification with the people launched a presentation of the message of personal salvation through Jesus Christ.

To follow the biblical example of Paul we first reach out to other people in their need and then build relationship through genuine shared interests. With Muslims, we can identify some of the parallels between the Bible and the Koran. With environmentalists, we share an appreciation of nature's beauty. With economists, we are interested in the market and money. To parents we talk about children. With athletes we talk sports. To gourmets we talk about great food. Paul knew and demonstrated that through authentic friendship and common ground there is often an opening for God.

Does it work? Not always. In Lystra, some of the people still wanted to worship Zeus and Hermes. The critics showed up. They were religious Jews who came nearly 100 miles from Antioch and Iconium to stir up trouble. They manipulated and persuaded the pagans against the missionaries.

> Then some Jews came from Antioch and Iconium and won the crowd over. They stoned Paul and dragged him outside the city, thinking he was dead. But after the disciples had gathered around him, he got up and went back into the city. The next day he and Barnabas left for Derbe. (14:19-20)

One minute they were worshiped as gods; the next they were stoned as demons. Stoning is vicious, and the intended result is the slow and agonizing death of the victim. Heavy rocks gashed, bloodied, bruised, and crushed the body. In this case no legal process was offered. This was gang brutality. Having completed their violence and believing Paul dead, the mob dragged him outside the city. It may have been to dispose of his body or they may have realized they had broken Roman law by murdering a Roman citizen, which could put them in very serious trouble with the authorities.

Paul was beaten but not quite dead. When he regained consciousness he got up and walked back into Lystra to show his would-be assassins that God had protected his life. He was courageous for the sake of Jesus.

But what good did it do? There is no report of thousands believing the message. There is no New Testament book written to the church at Lystra. Was this very different approach to evangelism a failure? Look again at a very important pair of words near the end of this story: "But after *the disciples* had gathered around him, he got up and went back into the city" (14:20, italics added). Paul had won the hearts of new disciples in Lystra. He and Barnabas had entered a city where not one Christian believer resided. Now they were leaving behind a seed of faith to grow and flourish.

Paul and Barnabas faced the people that Christians often have the hardest time speaking to—individuals antagonistic or indifferent to the Christian message. Today we have many opportunities to communicate with individuals of different faiths and backgrounds, but we often prefer to avoid this discomfort. Like the ancient missionaries, we will find comfort and possibility when we follow Jesus' lead: fill physical human need, glorify God, find common ground, and stand up again when beaten down.

Reflect and Discuss

1. In what ways was it easier for Paul and Barnabas to talk with unbelievers than it is for us today? In what ways was it more difficult?

2. What modern scenario would be comparable to the one that these disciples faced?

3. What interests and knowledge has God given you to share as you build authentic relationships with others?

CHAPTER 15

DARING TO CHANGE

(ACTS 15:1-21)

A cts 15 is one of the most important chapters in the Bible. It details a crisis that almost escalated into a war within the church, but in the end the Jesus followers made a critical decision—a change in direction that made all the difference to its future. Had Paul, Peter, Barnabas, and James not prevailed, the church would not be here today to share the hope available through Jesus Christ. There's a lesson here for modern Christians. The story starts with troublemakers.

God was accomplishing amazing work through the church at Antioch. People were turning to belief in Jesus. Spiritual growth increased daily. Giving was generous. Missionaries were being sent out to start new churches.

Then a group of self-appointed critics showed up to argue that the church was teaching a watered-down theology. These weren't the usual persecutors but fellow Christians. They insisted that no one could receive salvation through Jesus without first becoming a Jew. They argued that the teaching of Paul was cheap salvation and unscriptural. They preached that the church needed to teach a stricter approach, to raise its standards on who became a Christian, and to return to a straight and narrow path. "Some men came down from Judea to Antioch and were teaching the brothers: 'Unless you are circumcised, according to the custom taught by Moses, you cannot be saved.' This brought Paul and Barnabas into sharp dispute and debate with them" (15:1-2). Paul was angry and fought back, defending his teaching with the ardor that you would expect of this devoted disciple of Jesus. But the troublemakers were so persuasive they even convinced Peter they were right.

Read more of Paul's thoughts on the mess caused by the agitators in Galatians 2. He not only blasted the critics but also called the Apostle Peter a flip-flopper and a hypocrite. He reminded Peter that he once took a strong stand against Jewish Christians who insisted on Gentiles first becoming Jews. Back then Peter hung out with Gentiles and scandalized observant Jews by eating dinner in Gentile houses. Now, suddenly, Peter was won over to the side of narrow-minded teaching. Even steadfast Barnabas began to be swayed to their way of thinking.

This small group of divisive individuals almost derailed the church of Jesus Christ. They sounded reasonable, but by promoting a salvation-plus-circumcision gospel, they undermined the blessing and teaching of the Holy Spirit. There's a powerful principle here for Christians. Don't be troublemakers and don't follow the troublemakers. Be cautious and prayerful when others are inflammatory. Today, especially, our defenses need to be raised because of the power of newspapers, magazines, radio, television, blogs, email, and the Internet. Just because somebody—even another believer—says or writes something doesn't mean it's true.

To stop the trouble, the Antioch church appealed to the church in Jerusalem. At that time it was the "mother church," where Christianity began. The Jerusalem church called a council to debate and decide this very important issue. This council was not a democracy of all church members. It was a conference of church leaders that met for a very long discussion, with speeches, debate, and Bible study.

The Pharisees spoke first. They were devout Bible students who profoundly disagreed with Paul. It wasn't that they were opposed to Gentiles becoming Christians, but they argued they had to become Jews too—get circumcised, keep the law, and convert to Judaism in order to belong to the Christian church: "The Gentiles must be circumcised and required to obey the law of Moses" (15:5b).

They actually made some sense. They didn't want just anybody to become a Christian. They didn't want the Jewish Scriptures ignored or disobeyed.

Acts 15 summarizes the three speeches delivered by the Christians who held to Jesus' gospel message. Peter went first. Apparently his mind had been changed since he was in Antioch. I respect Peter for listening to reason and the Holy Spirit. Now he argued coherently about this important issue.

"Brothers, you know that some time ago God made a choice among you that the Gentiles might hear from my lips the message of the gospel and believe. God, who knows the heart, showed that he accepted them by giving the Holy Spirit to them, just as he did to us. He made no distinction between us and them, for he purified their hearts by faith. Now then, why do you try to test God by putting on the necks of the disciples a yoke that neither we nor our fathers have been able to bear? No! We believe it is through the grace of our Lord Jesus that we are saved, just as they are." (15:7b-11)

In the end Peter came to the supernatural realization that the only way to salvation is through the "grace of our Lord Jesus Christ" and not by following any set of religious rules.

Next, Barnabas and Paul spoke and they wowed the crowd: "The whole assembly became silent as they listened to Barnabas and Paul telling about the miraculous signs and wonders God had done among the Gentiles through them" (15:12). (It is interesting that Barnabas' name is listed first—probably because he was better known and trusted by the Christians in Jerusalem.) They didn't argue theology. They simply described what God was doing. Success is never the only measure of truth, but God's blessing is a powerful indicator.

Finally, James had his turn. He was the spiritual leader of the Jerusalem church and the brother of Jesus who once refused to believe but later became a Christian. This was a man of deep conviction. Jesus had made a special resurrection appearance just to James (1 Corinthians 15:7). He had several interesting nicknames including James the Just (because he was such a good man) and Camel Knees (because he spent so much time on his knees praying that his knees started looking like a camel's). James began by acknowledging the blessings of God on Gentile believers. He quoted the prophet Amos (9:11-12), giving evidence that God always intended to save the Gentiles, and not just the Jews.

"It is my judgment, therefore, that we should not make it difficult for the Gentiles who are turning to God. Instead we should write to them, telling them to abstain from food polluted by idols, from sexual immorality, from the meat of strangled animals and from blood. For Moses has been preached in every city from the earliest times and is read in the synagogues on every Sabbath." (15:19-21)

He concluded that they "should not make it difficult" for Gentiles to become Christians. As a man of common sense, James finally called on Gentile believers to respect certain Jewish traditions, especially in places where there were established synagogues alongside new Christian churches.

The decision of the Council was made and the troublemakers were dealt a major defeat. What a change for the Jerusalem church! From that day forward, the church was thrown wide open to everybody, Jewish or not, circumcised or not.

Did the first-century church immediately change as God designed? It did not. The old ways died hard. The conflicts continued. You can read all about the ongoing battle for the soul of the church in the rest of the New Testament. And, in too many ways, the controversy continues.

Like the first-century church, we must decide if we truly believe our God to be a God of grace and inclusiveness. Is our view of the gospel wide or narrow, generous or strict, based on grace or law? Jesus made it clear. This is not to say that anything goes and all beliefs lead to God. Nothing could be farther from what Jesus and the New Testament teach. The gospel is based on one way to God and eternal life through faith in Jesus as Savior. But it's faith in Jesus only, not Jesus plus the law, not Jesus plus a list of rules, not Jesus plus baptism, not Jesus plus good works, not Jesus plus church membership, not Jesus plus a particular denomination, not Jesus plus *anything*. Saint Paul wrote it better than anyone in Ephesians 2:8-9: "For it is by grace you have been saved, through faith—and this not from yourselves, it is the gift of God—not by works, so that no one can boast."

The grace of our Lord Jesus is outrageously generous—revolutionary. It is God's truth for us to believe and proclaim. Like those first Christians we can wholeheartedly grasp—and share—grace, but we are called to offer it as unadorned as Paul, Peter, and the other followers did. Simple grace can change our world.

Reflect and Discuss

1. Christians today still struggle with the temptation to add to the gospel. What are modern-day examples of "salvation plus"?

2. Do you struggle with "only Jesus" Christianity? In what ways?

3. What Bible verses remind you of the centrality of grace alone?

CHAPTER 16

ALIGNING WITH GOD'S VISION

(ACTS 16:6-10)

In the middle of the first century, Paul made a decision during a road trip that changed his life and the course of Christianity. At the time it may not have seemed like an important choice, but it was a turning point for the church.

> Paul and his companions traveled throughout the region of Phrygia and Galatia, having been kept by the Holy Spirit from preaching the word in the province of Asia. When they came to the border of Mysia, they tried to enter Bithynia, but the Spirit of Jesus would not allow them to. So they passed by Mysia and went down to Troas. (16:6-8)

How strange. Paul and the team wanted to do good by preaching the gospel, inviting people to become followers of Jesus, and establishing churches, but they were "kept by the Holy Spirit from preaching the word in the province of Asia." Paul and his colleagues walked hundreds of miles trying to figure out where God wanted them to go, but their way always seemed blocked.

The Holy Spirit stopped them from evangelizing! Certainly it wasn't because God didn't want the people of Asia to hear the gospel and become Christians. Rather, it was because the Holy

> *Paul's road trip took him through Asia, an area we now call Turkey, one of the Roman provinces. Jesus was born, crucified, and raised to life in Asia. It's where the church began. Followers of Jesus were first called Christians there. The explosion in the number of Christians and churches led by Saint Paul all occurred in Asia. For years, Christianity was an Asian religion. But Jesus had told his followers to be his witnesses "in Jerusalem, and in all Judea and Samaria, and to the ends of the earth" (Acts 1:8). The dream and vision of Jesus was a global church that would change every people, nation, continent, and culture.*

Spirit had a bigger global strategy and was positioning Paul and his team for something more important. His story is a reminder that when we try our best for God and it doesn't work, we shouldn't give up! God often uses closed doors to get us moved toward open doors. No is not a bad word from God. We may get a hundred nos on our journey to the divine yes.

How did Paul get God's direction through all these frustrating blockades? There is no indication that God spoke out loud and told him to take a different road. Instead, things just didn't work out, so he moved on. God does the same for us. You apply to a university and get rejected, so you know God wants you to apply elsewhere. You date someone you envision marrying but break up and ask someone else out. You pursue a job that will make your dreams come true and someone else gets it, so you apply for another job. It's not easy to have a door shut in your face, especially when God is doing the slamming. But if you truly trust God, you assume he knows something you don't. Another solution lies ahead.

What most impresses me about Paul and his team is that they kept moving. They didn't wait at home for God to call. Paul kept moving and we should too. Keep moving; keep looking; keep trying.

There's a clue to his seemingly endless journey in the fact that Paul got very sick on his first trip to this region with what may have been malaria.[1] Malaria is a recurring illness with chills, fever, light-headedness, shortness of breath, nausea, and other unpleasant symptoms. It can be fatal. Perhaps Paul didn't go to the places he was headed to because he kept getting sick. In Acts 16, Paul first met Luke, a physician who joined the team. If Paul was chronically ill, it would be wise to have a doctor as a fellow traveler. Perhaps Paul was on the lookout for a place and climate that provided relief. Even saints get sick. Christians are not exempt from medical problems—or any other kinds of problems, for that matter.

God used Paul's illness for good. If malaria was the tool of the Holy Spirit to get Paul and his team to Europe, then it must be said that his fever, nausea, and headaches were worth it. God often uses difficulty in our lives to get us where he wants us. When you feel lousy, remember that God can, ultimately, use bad health and awful days to bless you and make you an encouragement to others.

Still wandering, Paul and the team came to Troas on the Aegean Sea and at the western end of Asia. There was no hint that this would be anything other than another frustratingly short stay and closed door. I imagine Paul went to bed that night, discouraged, thinking, "God, is this it? Is this all you had in mind for me, this endless walking?" It's hard when you try your hardest and nothing works, and it's even more depressing when you are sick. I wonder if Paul thought about quitting his missionary expeditions that night in Troas. But God had a message for him, one that would change his mind—and his course. "During the night Paul had a vision of a man of Macedonia standing and begging him, 'Come over to Macedonia and help us.' After Paul had seen the vision, we got ready at once to leave for Macedonia, concluding that God had called us to preach the gospel to them" (16:9-10).

Paul could have interpreted this vision any way he wanted. He could have blamed it on the fever from malaria or on his discouragement and desperation causing him to hallucinate or on bad seafood. But Paul attributed the vision to God. Paul was looking. Paul was ready.

The Macedonian man's words were enough to get his imagination working. He could take a boat across the Hellespont (the

Dardanelles) to Macedonia. There might be a synagogue where he could share the gospel of Jesus with the people. Maybe a church could be established in Europe. This could be the start of something significant. I'm glad he had a chance to work through this concept on his own. In brainstorming sessions there are always some who, in response to a brave, new idea ask, "What if it doesn't work?" Paul seemed to be asking the opposite question: "What if it does work? What if Europe says yes to Jesus?"

Others soon adopted Paul's God-given dream. Luke, the author of the Gospel of Luke and of the book of Acts, became Paul's fellow visionary. In the first fifteen chapters of Acts, he wrote like any objective reporter and historian. Then something subtle but significant occurred. Notice the change in pronouns between verses 8 and 10: "So *they* passed by Mysia and went down to Troas.... After Paul had seen the vision, *we* got ready at once to leave for Macedonia, concluding that God had called *us* to preach the gospel to them" (italics added).

Luke switched from bystander to participant, from physician to missionary, from reporter to evangelist. This was now *his* vision, *his* mission, and *his* passion too. This was a historic turning point for Christianity and for Luke. He joined the team, took responsibility, and committed himself. That morning in Troas, Luke switched from involvement to commitment in the church and cause of Jesus. Blessed are those who change from "they" to "we."

The vision to evangelize Europe was a first-century vision, and—because of Paul, Silas, Timothy, and Luke—the church was established in Europe and has continued to grow for over 2,000 years. Europe became the epicenter of the church of Jesus Christ.

That was the first century. In the twenty-first century, God has once again turned the world upside down. Look at these contrasts.

In 1900, 70 percent of the Christians in the world lived in Europe. By 2000, 28 percent of world Christians lived in Europe.

In 1900, there were 10 million Christians in Africa. In 2000, there were 360 million Christians in Africa.[2]

In 1900, 90 percent of the world's Christians lived in North America, Europe, Australia, and New Zealand. Only 10 percent of the Christians lived in the non-Western world. In 2000, 70 percent or more of the world's Christians lived in the non-Western world. Today there are more Christians who belong to Anglican churches in Nigeria than in all the Episcopal and Anglican churches of Britain, Europe, and North America combined. There are more Baptists in the Congo than in Great Britain. There are more Christians worshiping in the churches of communist China each Sunday than in all of Western Europe combined. The Assemblies of God have ten times more members in Latin America than in the United States.[3]

God crossed continents to win his world to Jesus in Bible times and God is crossing continents to win generations to Jesus in our times.

Every day we make hundreds of decisions, large and small. Most of them are forgotten quickly and have little impact, but there are some decisions that shape and define our lives and the lives of others forever. What's your vision from God? What would he like to do through you that would make a genuine difference? Serve the poor? Share the gospel with a coworker? Give generously and sacrificially? Pray effectively? Teach children? Become a missionary? What do you dream about for God? What is your big, courageous, wild adventure for Jesus Christ? Like Paul we can always search, always believe, and always respond when God gives the go-ahead to a vision for the future of God's church.

Reflect and Discuss

1. How did Paul align himself with God's vision for the church?

2. Paul's decision to take the message of Jesus into new countries resulted in a global church. How can you assist in this effort using your gifts?

3. Has God used hardship or disappointment to help you remain open to his leading? How well did you cope with the difficulties?

CHAPTER 17

PERSEVERING IN THE WORST CIRCUMSTANCES

(ACTS 16:13-40)

Four men—Paul, Timothy, Silas, and Luke—disembarked from a trans-Aegean voyage at the seaport of Neapolis and walked ten miles along the Via Egnatia, a famed Roman-built road. Their destination was the city of Philippi, a city in northern Greece. By now travel was a way of life for these disciples of Jesus.

They arrived in Philippi by midweek and asked around for the local Jewish synagogue, where they intended to teach. They must have been surprised to discover that there was no synagogue in town—unusual for a city of this size. Never easily discouraged from their mission, the men went in search of another likely gathering spot for people seeking conversation about spiritual matters. Luke recorded the story of a significant encounter:

> On the Sabbath we went outside the city gate to the river, where we expected to find a place of prayer. We sat down and began to speak to the women who had gathered there. One of those listening was a woman named Lydia, a dealer in purple cloth from the city of Thyatira, who was a worshiper of God. (16:13-14a)

Of all cloth colors, purple was one of the most desirable and expensive. It was made by extracting drops of pigment from a special shellfish. One pound of purple cloth sold for the equivalent of hundreds of our dollars.[1] This was a person high on the socioeconomic scale—successful, well-to-do, influential, and seeking God.

> The Lord opened her heart to respond to Paul's message. When she and the members of her household were baptized, she invited us to her home. "If you consider me a believer in the Lord," she said, "come and stay at my house." And she persuaded us. (16:14b-15)

Lydia became the first recorded Christian in Europe. Thereafter, her home, which was no doubt large and well furnished, became the meetinghouse for the church of Philippi. Why did Luke include her story in his writings? Paul had made thousands of converts to the Christian faith and could have told a thousand stories. Lydia's story is an encouragement and model for people like her—those who are successful, wealthy, and well known.

But God never intended the church to be only for the rich and successful. The next recorded convert gives us a completely different picture. "Once when we were going to the place of prayer, we were met by a slave girl who had a spirit by which she predicted the future. She earned a great deal of money for her owners by fortune-telling" (16:16).

Slaves, a mainstay of Roman life and the Roman economy, comprised a significant percentage of the population in the empire. Bought and sold for hard labor, teaching, business, prostitution, and household chores, slaves were under the absolute control of their owners. This particular girl's owners had discovered a way to exploit her, selling her services as a fortune-teller and predictor of the future. Perhaps her owners were attracted to the crowds drawn to the disciples because the girl "followed Paul and the rest of us, shouting, 'These men are servants of the Most High God, who are telling you the way to be saved.' She kept this up for many days" (16:17-18). It went on for days. Her shouts must have made people stop in their tracks. Salvation—a desire to escape the anger of the gods—was a popular issue of the time.

The girl was possessed by an evil spirit—a demon. To modern readers, this might seem like superstitious nonsense. Our culture has underplayed the presence and power of demons, but they still exist and continue to exercise power over people. Demons are smart enough to fit into our sophisticated society and work so that they are not always recognized. Their power is very real.

Why a demon would advertise the gospel is hard to explain—unless it was expected that the endorsement might discredit the gospel. Paul put up with it for a long while, but finally he "became so troubled that he turned around and said to the spirit, 'In the name of Jesus Christ I command you to come out of her!' At that moment the spirit left her" (16:18).

Paul showed great compassion by healing this girl. We don't learn from Luke whether, released from the bondage of her affliction, the girl understood and believed the message proclaimed by the disciples, but it certainly seems possible. This is the story of a destitute girl being touched by the gospel and grace of Jesus.

As soon as her owners realized their source of income had been cut off, they were outraged. They dragged Paul and Silas into the marketplace to face criminal charges: "They brought them before the magistrates and said, 'These men are Jews, and are throwing our city into an uproar by advocating customs unlawful for us Romans to accept or practice'" (16:20-21).

The first words against Paul and Silas were "these men are Jews." Today we would call it profiling, racism, or anti-Semitism. The accusers didn't use evidence to spark their controversy; they used prejudice. Luke wrote, "The crowd joined in the attack" (16:22). The fuel for the fire came next—an accusation of anarchy. Paul and Silas were said to be unpatriotic and promoting un-Roman practices.

With the crowd shouting for conviction, the magistrates jumped to a quick verdict and sentence. Paul and Silas were stripped naked in public and severely flogged until they were raw, swollen, and bleeding. Jewish people were typically very modest, so the humiliation of being naked was probably as painful as the beating.

Treating them as if they were high-value terrorists instead of teachers and miracle-workers, the magistrates ordered maximum-security imprisonment. The jailer shackled them into stocks that clamped down their feet, hands, and maybe even their heads. They were locked in a dungeon, where there were no windows or light. They were locked behind multiple doors and heavy guard. In those days food was not provided in prison. Someone on the outside had to bring it in or the prisoner went hungry. This was torture.

What do you do when beaten, shackled, hungry, thirsty, and isolated? The disciples' response was unique. "About midnight Paul and Silas were praying and singing hymns to God, and the other prisoners were listening to them" (16:25). Even in the worst of circumstances Paul and Silas demonstrated their faith and the grace of God.

Around midnight, while they were singing, a violent earthquake shook Philippi. It reached to the foundations of the prison, broke the stocks and shackles and smashed open all the prison doors and gates. The warden of the prison was asleep until the earthquake started. He woke up in a panic. His prisoners were free and the night shift of guards could not keep them from escaping. Under Roman law, the warden was fully responsible regardless of the reason. If prisoners escaped, the jailer received their sentence as punishment. If they all escaped he was subject to every beating, torture, and execution of all the inmates combined. He quickly concluded that suicide was his best option. He drew his sword and was ready to kill himself when the prisoner from the deepest dungeon shouted to him. It was Paul, who yelled, "Don't harm yourself! We are all here!" (16:28).

Prisoners staying voluntarily in an unlocked jail was about as likely as air staying in a punctured balloon. But somehow the warden sensed truth in Paul's voice even though the lights were out and he couldn't be sure. He called for torches to be lit, saw for himself that everyone was present, and ran to Paul and Silas. He fell at their feet, trembling. Bringing them into the light, he asked the most important question of his life: "Sirs, what must I do to be saved?" (16:30).

It was a question with many possible interpretations. What did he need to do to be saved from the earthquake? From all the prisoners escaping and being held accountable? From sin and for

God? Whatever he was asking, Paul and Silas gave the answer to every question: "Believe in the Lord Jesus, and you will be saved—you and your household" (16:31).

The jailer asked some questions and got some teaching. It didn't take long. He and his whole household believed. They were baptized that same night. He not only survived the ordeal but also was transformed from suicidal fear to unexpected joy. "He was filled with joy because he had come to believe in God—he and his whole family" (16:34).

He wasn't rich and upper-class like Lydia or poor and demon possessed like the slave girl. He was a middle-class civil servant doing his job. The disciples showed that the gospel of Jesus wasn't based on class, gender, job, slavery, or freedom. All people were sinners and Jesus died and was resurrected to save them all.

The morning after the earthquake, the local magistrates had second thoughts about beating and jailing Paul and Silas. They ordered them released and asked them to leave the city. Even with their abrupt departure, much had been accomplished during this leg of their journey. Not only had hearts been opened to Jesus, but the disciples had shown that he was for all people. The church penetrated every level of society, from the rich to poor to middle-class. Jesus' church was for everybody.

Modern-day Christians can also grow the church of Jesus to include everybody—rich, poor, young, old, male, female, famous, forgotten, native, immigrant. Everybody. The message to them all is "believe in the Lord Jesus, and you will be saved."

Reflect and Discuss

1. In what ways is it hard for Christians today to include everybody as they tell the good news of Jesus?

2. Imagine yourself in the place of Paul and Silas in prison—in pain, hungry, parched, and lonely. What would be your response?

3. What changes would need to occur in your life in order to praise God despite the suffering?

CONFRONTING CHALLENGES WITH HOPE

(ACTS 18)

W hat does it take to live and speak for Jesus in tough times and inhospitable places? Christians need to know the answer to that question because sooner or later we will all find ourselves in that position. Acts 18 offers guidance based on Paul's continuing work to establish the church. The year was AD 49 and the place was Corinth. Luke recorded Paul's journey to this city about 65 miles southwest of Athens. In comparison to Athens—a sophisticated university town with about 10,000 population—Corinth was a wild commercial metropolis of almost 750,000 people. The city was the third largest in the Roman Empire and a major overland commercial and shipping center. The city had been destroyed by the Romans in 146 BC and then rebuilt in splendor by Julius Caesar in 44 BC.

Corinth was diverse—with Jews, Romans, Greeks, slaves, and freed slaves from all over the Mediterranean world. Freed slaves were a major part of the population, many of them having been sent from overpopulated Rome to get a fresh start in a major boom city. Imagine the excitement of visiting a metropolis where such a broad mixture of races, languages, ethnicities, and religions mingled.

Corinth was also famous for its overt immorality. The term "to Corinthianize" meant to engage in promiscuous sex and debauchery. The city was at the base of the 1,886 foot high Acrocorinth with its temple to the goddess Aphrodite at the top. Aphrodite was the Greek goddess of sexual love and beauty. The Romans called her Venus. It is reported that the temple of Aphrodite had one thousand prostitute priestesses who came down off the mountain at night to work the streets of Corinth until morning. In Greek plays the Corinthian characters were often depicted as drunk.[1]

Put it all together and you have a picture of a tough place to start a church, yet there was Paul. He stayed and worked in Corinth for almost two years—longer than most of the places he went. He didn't complain or give up in disgust. He just kept laboring.

> After this, Paul left Athens and went to Corinth. There he met a Jew named Aquila, a native of Pontus, who had recently come from Italy with his wife Priscilla, because Claudius had ordered all the Jews to leave Rome. Paul went to see them, and because he was a tentmaker as they were, he stayed and worked with them. Every Sabbath he reasoned in the synagogue, trying to persuade Jews and Greeks.
>
> When Silas and Timothy came from Macedonia, Paul devoted himself exclusively to preaching, testifying to the Jews that Jesus was the Christ. (18:1-5)

In his bestselling business book, *Good to Great,* Jim Collins says that one of the primary responsibilities of great leaders of successful companies is getting "the right people on the bus, the wrong people off the bus, and the right people in the right seats."[2] When Paul recruited Aquila and Priscilla, he got the right people on the bus for Jesus Christ. They had lived around the empire, were Jewish in background, and grounded in their faith. Exiled from Rome by the Emperor Claudius as part of an early first-century persecution, they, like Paul, were tentmakers by profession. He moved into their home, worked in their shop, and invited them onto his church-planting team. It was one of the best decisions Paul ever made.

Veteran team members Silas and Timothy caught up with Paul in Corinth. What a blessing they were. Paul knew the churches he was seeding needed godly leaders, solid in their faith and knowledge of Scripture. Many Corinthians had so many issues and so little background in Scripture that it was critically important their leaders be spiritually fit and wise. He got the right people on the bus in the right seats. Silas and Timothy were able to take over some of Paul's responsibilities so he could devote himself full-time to preaching. They brought money given by the churches to the north so that Paul could quit his job as a tentmaker.

Paul started teaching in the synagogue of Corinth. However, some of the Jews in the synagogue started complaining, criticizing, and opposing Paul and his Christian message. There is nothing that detracts Christians from reaching a goal and fulfilling a mission more than critics. On one hand, no leader dares be so arrogant as to ignore critics; on the other, any leader who continually accommodates critics and complainers never gets anything done.

Churches and Christians face the same challenge today. Every church and organization has people who are unhappy and want to voice their opposition. Leaders must do whatever they need to do to get back to the mission of reaching people for Jesus.

That's what Paul did. In essence, his message to critics was, "You've got a problem. I did the best I could. It's still your problem, and I'm out of here." Luke wrote that Paul "shook out his clothes in protest and said to them, 'Your blood be on your own heads! I am clear of my responsibility. From now on I will go to the Gentiles' " (18:6). Paul wasn't about to let their abuse and dysfunction divert him from the goal of making new Christians.

Not all of the Jews were abusive. He walked out of the synagogue and started a church next door in a private home. Crispus was the president of the synagogue and he became a Christian, along with his family and employees. Paul went with the responsive individuals and left the rest.

It may sound like Paul lacked compassion. To the contrary, he had great compassion but couldn't waste his time with the troublemakers and ignore those who were interested in the message of Jesus Christ. We should do the same. There comes a time to just move on.

Paul made excellent leadership decisions—a first-century model for the twenty-first century who knew that no matter what his skills were, it was God's divine blessing that made the real difference.

One night the Lord spoke to Paul in a vision: "Do not be afraid; keep on speaking, do not be silent. For I am with you, and no one is going to attack and harm you, because I have many people in this city." So Paul stayed for a year and a half, teaching them the word of God. (18:9-11)

Remember that these wonderfully encouraging words from Jesus came after Paul was criticized, undermined, and abused. He had already persevered through difficulty before he received further encouragement not to give up.

Jesus often works this way with us too. We are faithful even when life is hard; then Jesus encourages us to persevere some more.

In the provincial Roman court, Paul's Jewish critics organized and brought him before the proconsul Gallio. " 'This man,' they charged, 'is persuading the people to worship God in ways contrary to the law' " (18:13). To understand the charges we need to know how Roman law dealt with religion. Unlike most ancient empires, the Romans did not force those they conquered to adopt Roman religion. Legal religions were called *religio licita*; illegal religions were called *religio illicita*. The Jews were arguing that Judaism was *religio licita* and that Paul was introducing a new religion that was *religio illicita*. If they prevailed before the proconsul, Christianity would immediately be illegal and churches shut down—a pivotal moment in church history.

God moved the heart and mind of this powerful politician. Gallio dismissed the case without even hearing Paul's defense.

This ruling immediately legalized Christianity—not only in the province of Achaia but also everywhere in the Roman Empire.

Paul's critics were so upset with the court ruling that they turned on their new synagogue president, Sosthenes, and beat him in front of the proconsul's quarters but "Gallio showed no concern whatever" (18:17b).

It's a good thing Paul didn't skip Corinth just because he discovered it was a tough assignment. He didn't quit even when criticized, abused, and hauled to court. He hung in there. Paul was so encouraged by God's blessing and the response to Jesus that he stayed in Corinth for two years and later wrote four letters back to the Corinthian church, two of which are part of our New Testament today.

The rest of Acts 18 is a short sequel to the story from Corinth. When Paul finally left the city, he gave top priority to having the right people in the right places. Silas and Timothy remained in Corinth; Priscilla and Aquila went with Paul to get started in Ephesus; and they recruited Apollos. Articulate, educated, godly, and ready for discipling, Apollos had great potential in Paul's eyes. He was sent back to Achaia to develop the new churches and Christians in Corinth and Athens.

Paul kept moving. His mission was to start new churches and strengthen established ones. He revisited the churches previously started to check up on them and strengthen them. He returned to his home church of Antioch to report all God was doing and renew the people's support. Paul was one of those Christians who knew what God wanted him to do and did it.

The sequel has a strange scene in which Paul shaved his head and took a vow. There was an ancient Jewish tradition of shaving one's head, saving the hair, and abstaining from alcohol until it grew back. When the hair grew back, the saved hair was burned as a sacrifice to God. Sometimes the purpose was to seek God's blessing or to thank him for a blessing. Either way, Paul was keenly aware of the blessing of Jesus on his life and wanted to go on record as grateful. It is still good to recognize God's blessings and to celebrate those blessings with a significant act—perhaps a day of prayer and fasting or a special gift.

What would you do if faced with enormous challenges like Paul encountered? Would you respond with discouragement or hope? We are the twenty-first-century sequel to Paul's story when we enlist the help of godly colleagues, maintain a clear mission, and seek God's divine blessing on our efforts. We too can figure out what God wants us to do and—regardless of setbacks, disappointments, and opposition—do it.

Reflect and Discuss

1. Paul dealt with complainers. Do you feel pressure, sometimes, to listen to critics rather than accomplish God's work?

2. Consider how Paul worked his way through challenges and accomplished goals. What practical applications can you use in your own life?

3. What Hebrew Scriptures might Paul have relied on when confronting difficulties?

CHAPTER 19

MODELING THE WAY, NOT ARGUING

(ACTS 19:1-41)

P aul traveled to Ephesus, where he spent three months at the synagogue "arguing persuasively about the kingdom of God" (19:8). Some of the listeners at the synagogue became obstinate and belligerent enough to "publicly [malign] the Way" (19:9). (Followers of Jesus weren't known by the term "Christians" yet; the teachings and truth of Jesus were at first called "The Way."[1]) It's a scenario that may seem familiar to modern Christians. What should believers do when others seek to discredit them?

In Acts 19, the disciples didn't stick around for the abuse. They moved to a lecture hall, where they spent two years having lively discussions with both Jews and Greeks. It was a remarkable time. God used Paul in new and powerful ways. Even a handkerchief or apron touched by Paul could be used by others to cure illness or exorcise evil spirits.

It was a revolution. Belief in Jesus was sweeping Ephesus, challenging presuppositions and altering the prevalent pagan worldview. Luke reports that "the name of the Lord Jesus was held in high honor. Many of those who believed now came and openly confessed their evil deeds" (19:17b, 18). The miracles turned people to Jesus.

As often happens at the pinnacle of success, trouble again arrived. "About that time there arose a great disturbance about the Way" (19:23). This disturbance to the way things had always been done created understandable confusion and serious outrage. The buzz penetrated every part of this great city. People were talking and debating, and many were embracing this whole new way of life.

Trouble started when a silversmith named Demetrius called a rally of his fellow craftsmen and artisans from related fields. A talented maker of silver shrines of the goddess Artemis and her temple, he made a tidy profit selling his trinkets to local Ephesians and tourists. But changes occurring in the city were dramatically cutting into his sales. For financial reasons, he wanted the other workers to organize against this nonstop influence of The Way. Demetrius offered persuasive arguments and fearful consequences to sway the others to his side (19:24-27).

> *In ancient Ephesus visitors were awed by grand homes, magnificent in architecture and craftsmanship. The city was home to great art and an important library. It was also home to the stunningly beautiful temple of Artemis, the patron goddess of Ephesus, counted as one of the Seven Wonders of the Ancient World.*

It is easy to criticize Demetrius, but I'm not sure we are much different. When threatened with change, we are all prone to defend our jobs, money, and way of life. The silversmith guild gathered a crowd of critics and incited a riot. The crowd roared through the Arcadian Way, the central marble boulevard of Ephesus, chanting, "Great is Artemis of the Ephesians!" (19:28). Adrenaline was pumping. The shouts could be heard across the city. Newcomers joined in, even those who didn't know what the protest was about. People poured from their homes and followed the parade to the amphitheater at the foot of Mount Pion.

They grabbed Gaius and Aristarchus, colleagues of Paul, and dragged them into the city amphitheater, a huge enclosure that could seat 25,000. Hearing of the intense controversy, the Apostle Paul wanted to appear before the crowd, but the disciples, knowing the danger of violence, would not allow it. Even officials of the province—friends of Paul—sent him a message imploring him not to go into the amphitheater. It was chaos.

Ephesian Jews were afraid they would come under attack and wanted to distinguish themselves from the Christians before it was too late. They pushed one of their leaders, Alexander, onto the platform to explain that Jews were not Christians. He attempted to silence the crowd so he could reason with them, but when the crowd realized he was a Jew, they again started chanting thunderously, "Great is Artemis of the Ephesians!" It went on for two frenzied hours.

All this happened because the teaching of Jesus came to town.

But Christianity is about peace, not anarchy. It was intended by God to help people, not hurt them. The Ephesians misunderstood. The conflict arose from a clash of cultures. The Gospel of Jesus has the power to change people's behavior, outlook, and lives. Sometimes it comes into an environment and shifts priorities so the culture of self-indulgence that once existed fades.

When Christians are severely criticized by enemies who are making false, emotionally charged accusations, should they answer back? It's happened to many of us. I've been upset by people misrepresenting my words, intentions, and beliefs. They've flat out lied. I have been forced to wrestle with a difficult choice: should I defend myself or keep quiet?

Paul felt a strong urge to answer his critics face-to-face, even though they were worked into a frenzy. What did he plan to say? My guess is he would have avoided criticizing the silversmiths, condemning their trinkets, or attacking Artemis as a false god. He would have talked about Jesus.

However worthy his objective, Paul would have found himself over his head. Wise advisors told him to sit tight. Even some of the local politicos in Ephesus sent word that Paul should avoid speaking to the crowd. It would do no good and would put him in danger. Good advice. The mob at Ephesus was hysterical and frenzied. No matter what he said or did, they would turn it against him. It was one of those times when keeping quiet was the better approach. A nurse working on a dementia ward once told me, "You cannot have a rational conversation with an irrational person."

As Christians we must choose—is our message mostly against what's wrong in the culture or mostly for the good news of Jesus? Even when people are angry, agitated, or dead set against the message of Jesus Christ, we can influence our culture by living godly lives. We can be gentle in our response, speaking the truth of Jesus in love rather than in anger. We can treat our critics with respect. The godly traits of honesty, integrity, and transparency are persuasive. The ability to love others—especially in the face of opposition—is almost irresistible.

How can we live in a way that elevates Jesus?

- Know him intimately so that everything about you— your behavior, words, attitude—will be transformed.
- Pray constantly to see how this act changes you and the world around you.
- Be an advocate for the disadvantaged, ostracized, and weakest of society.
- Speak the truth of your faith at God-given opportunities.
- Love rather than judge.
- Sacrifice to help others.

The Christians of Ephesus decided not to argue, fight, or defend themselves against the crowd of critics. God honored their decision. What happened next was officially an action of a Roman politician, but it was clearly orchestrated by God. Respected and trusted by the people of Ephesus, the unnamed city clerk cautioned the crowd not to do anything rash (Acts 19:35-41). The riot ended with a whimper. The crowd melted away and everyone walked home and went to bed.

By recording this story of the riot in Ephesus, historian Luke made clear that Rome had no legal problem with Christianity. The

Empire of Rome and the kingdom of God had diametrically opposed worldviews, but they could live together in peace. Christians weren't out to overthrow the government but only to change people for good, one individual at a time.

As Christians who also want to offer God's peace to unbelievers, we must choose whom we work for—our own profit or Jesus Christ. Only when Jesus is at the center of our lives can we hope to influence our culture and world.

The goal courageously pursued by Paul and the Christians in Ephesus has not been fully achieved. It is now in the hands of twenty-first-century followers of The Way. We commit to spreading the word—sharing the good news with others—but an overthrow is not the goal. Love is. Service is. Justice is. Salvation is. We must live wholeheartedly for Jesus and allow him to change people as a result of what they see in us. We must live for Jesus in the easy places and the hard places, in the best of times and the worst of times. As we serve God and love people, our culture will be changed—without argument.

Reflect and Discuss

1. A nameless city clerk spoke reason to defuse the crowd's anger. This man was not a follower of Jesus, but his moral behavior greatly affected the outcome of the scene. What can be learned from this story?

2. Resistance to Christianity isn't always based on doctrinal or social issues. What does this story of Ephesus teach modern-day Christians about reaching nonbelievers?

3. Have you ever felt the urge to defend yourself when maligned—and then felt God's prompting to remain silent? What happened?

TREASURING THE FAMILY

(ACTS 20:13-38)

S aying goodbye can be agonizing, especially when you're parting from dear friends. In Acts 20, Paul bid an emotional farewell to the leaders of the church in Ephesus and his story reveals the depth and importance of connection between people who share faith in Jesus.

Paul and his party had concluded a fundraising trip and were on their way to deliver money to poor Christians in Jerusalem. They stopped for a week in the city of Troas on the eastern shore of the Aegean Sea, south of the modern city of Istanbul. Paul's original plan was to arrive in Jerusalem for the Jewish Passover, but he had been delayed by a threat on his life. Now he was aiming to arrive in Jerusalem seven weeks later for the Festival of Pentecost. While making his way there, he stopped in Miletus and sent word to the leaders of the Ephesus church to meet him. It was important that he see these friends again because of all they had been through together. They were more than friends; they were fellow survivors.

When the old friends arrived, I'm certain there were hugs and maybe tears of joy. Paul now addressed them as a group. His speech is fascinating because it is the only one recorded in the book of Acts delivered solely to Christians. All other talks were given to unbelievers or to a mixed audience of believers and unbelievers. Luke, the historian, focused mostly on outreach and evangelism in his writings because that's what the early church was all about, but now he switched gears. Notice how twice Luke reports Paul using the phrase "you know" because he was recounting shared memories, something we all do with old friends.

> "You know how I lived the whole time I was with you, from the first day I came into the province of Asia. I served the Lord with great humility and with tears, although I was severely tested by the plots of the Jews. You know that I have not hesitated to preach anything that would be helpful to you but have taught you publicly and from house to house. I have declared to both Jews and Greeks that they must turn to God in repentance and have faith in our Lord Jesus." (20:18-21)

Paul recalled the good and the bad, the easy and the difficult, the pleasant and the painful. It is sad that Paul had to remember so much pain, but that is reality for many believers. The Christian life is wonderful and rewarding but not always easy. By recalling honestly the trials they had endured together, Paul pointed to perseverance even when life was tough. Like Paul, we grow closer to the people who have experienced difficulty with us. Christians support and assist fellow believers through hardships.

Paul's farewell then switched from memories to anticipation. He said he was en route to Jerusalem where "the Holy Spirit warns me that prison and hardships are facing me" (20:23).

He sensed trouble to come. Perhaps a prophet in one of the churches warned him that his death was imminent. He certainly expected more of the harsh and inhumane treatment he had received during his earlier travels. He expected the worst, yet he coped by renewing his enthusiasm to spread the word of Jesus. He didn't know when his life would end but he was totally committed to faithfully preaching the gospel for as much time as he had left. Paul added a famous line often quoted by Christians today:

"I consider my life worth nothing to me, if only I may finish the race and complete the task the Lord Jesus has given me—the task of testifying to the gospel of God's grace" (20:24).

Giving his farewell exhortations to the leaders of the Ephesian church, Paul advised, "Keep watch over yourselves and all the flock of which the Holy Spirit has made you overseers" (20:28a). The Christian leaders were encouraged to grow their own souls and spiritual lives. The principle Paul was trying to express was similar to that invoked by flight attendants today when they instruct adults to put on their own oxygen masks before attempting to help the child sitting next to them. If you don't take care of yourself, you won't be able to help others.

Paul used a graphic illustration to help the leaders see how vital their role would be in the church. He said that "savage wolves will come in among you . . . and distort the truth in order to draw away disciples" (20:29, 30). As a mentor and leader of these church elders, he warned them to be on the lookout. His advice holds true today. One of the top jobs of church leaders is to protect fellow Christians from bad influences and people. Pastors think about this every day. There is a constant flow of people who want to teach their false ideas, sell their distracting materials, and promote their misleading programs in the church. Shepherds need to constantly be on guard.

Finally, Paul exhorted them to remember the words of Jesus, who said, "It is more blessed to give than to receive." He called for the church to give generously to others. This is a quote from Jesus that was never written into the Gospels but was passed to Paul who quoted it for the benefit and growth of his fellow believers. These words were to shape and anchor the church.

The "all aboard!" was shouted. The ship was sailing. Everyone present knew Paul would never come that way again. This was his last goodbye to those he had introduced to Jesus and the Christians he had discipled. The scene ended with great emotion. "When he had said this, he knelt down with all of them and prayed. They all wept as they embraced him and kissed him. What grieved them most was his statement that they would never see his face again. Then they accompanied him to the ship" (20:36-38).

Paul's goodbye shows us that the special link between followers of Jesus has existed from the beginning—and continues to this day. Those who have experienced friendship with other Christians have felt the emotional and spiritual attachment that Paul felt that day. These are no ordinary friendships. The connection is deep, personal, and spiritual.

We are reminded that the church is a community of people who deeply love and care for one another. It is made up of people who pray with us, weep for us, and become community and family.

We might read this segment of Acts purely as a biography of a saint—a man much different from us in his ability to serve God. But this is more. It is an encouragement for all Christians. We will all die. When and how is beyond our final control, but we can run the race for Jesus to the end—and with the prayers, encouragement, and understanding of fellow Christians who share the same quest on earth.

Someday you may be saying goodbye to a fellow believer and feel the ache that Paul endured at the dock of Miletus. Take comfort. Because we are Christians, there is never a final goodbye. We are promised the ultimate reunion of eternal life with Jesus.

Reflect and Discuss

1. Luke included just one passage describing Paul's preaching to fellow believers. Why is it included? Why do you suppose there are no other sections like it?

2. How are your friendships with Christians different from other friendships?

3. Name a few friendships that are described in the Bible. What can you learn about God's plan for Christian friends from these descriptions?

CHAPTER 21

REAPING UNDESERVED GOOD

(ACTS 21:1-16)

W hat happens when people reject the good counsel of family, friends, teachers, lawyers, counselors, and physicians? Our sense of justice says they must end up in disaster, right? Not always. Sometimes people ignore the best advice in the world and everything still works out fine.

Who would ever guess that Saint Paul would be one of those stubborn, bull-headed people who ignored good advice and did what he wanted to do anyway? Paul and eight of his friends had left the dock at Miletus and were heading to Jerusalem to deliver the relief money to poor Christians in Jerusalem. Acts 21 is Luke's trip journal reporting their travels. He acted as the group photographer before cameras were invented. He tells us about their travels from Miletus to Tyre—more than 500 miles by sea— with the stops and sites along the way.

The first decision of Paul and his friends was to connect with the local Christians in Tyre, an important city and seaport. When Paul and his team left a week later, they were spiritually bonded. These new brothers and sisters in Jesus walked them out of the city, kneeled down and prayed with them, and then watched as the disciples boarded the boat and sailed away.

But the Tyre believers had a message for Paul. They warned him not to go to Jerusalem because it was too dangerous. "Through the Spirit they urged Paul not to go on to Jerusalem" (21:4). This wasn't just their opinion or feeling. The Holy Spirit spoke through them: cancel the trip to Jerusalem; it's ill-advised and will end in disaster. Luke does not report Paul's response, but obviously he decided to ignore their pleas for he was soon back on the boat.

> We continued our voyage from Tyre and landed at Ptolemais, where we greeted the brothers and stayed with them for a day. Leaving the next day, we reached Caesarea and stayed at the house of Philip the evangelist, one of the Seven. (21:7-8)

There are several Philips in the New Testament, including one who was an apostle and one of Jesus' original twelve disciples. But this is the Philip chosen as one of the seven key leaders of the Jerusalem church, twenty years earlier. He handled money for widows (6:5). When forced to flee Jerusalem under persecution, Philip went to Samaria and evangelized thousands, performing many miracles (8:5-13). Philip was the evangelist who led the Ethiopian eunuch to faith in Jesus (8:26-38). He eventually settled in Caesarea and was so successful in sharing the good news of Jesus and bringing new believers into the church that he was nick-named "the Evangelist." Paul was a greatly blessed Christian leader, but Philip was clearly his peer and spiritual equal.

Philip had four unmarried daughters who grew up in Caesarea and became prophets. In the New Testament church, prophecy was a primary gift of leadership. The gift included prediction of the future but was primarily teaching the truth of God to the Christians in the church. It is impressive that one family produced four prophets and noteworthy that these four women are mentioned in leadership and teaching roles. They were part of a male-dominated society that often disrespected and oppressed women. Obviously the church valued and respected these women. Since Luke mentioned them, it seems likely that they too warned Paul not to go to Jerusalem.

While on their layover in Caesarea, Paul was visited by yet another prophet from Judea—Agabus—who made a memorable point through a dramatic presentation.

> "Coming over to us, he took Paul's belt, tied his own hands and feet with it and said, 'The Holy Spirit says, "In this way the Jews of Jerusalem will bind the owner of this belt and will hand him over to the Gentiles." ' When we heard this, we and the people there pleaded with Paul not to go up to Jerusalem" (21:11-12).

So Paul was not-so-subtly advised not to go to Jerusalem. He heard from prophets, individuals, and groups, who implored him to give up his plans. Luke wrote that God, the Holy Spirit himself, directly warned him against going. The message could not have been clearer.

And what did Paul decide to do? He went to Jerusalem. Why? He wanted to go. He was a driven man, unafraid of prison or death. He was a godly man who wanted to be like Jesus, who also went to Jerusalem under threat of death. Nothing anyone could say would dissuade him.

Imagine that you are a friend of Paul. In your heart you know that his plans are dangerous—maybe even deadly. You've heard wise fellow Christians mirror your concerns. And yet Paul remains stubbornly determined to leave you and go into Jerusalem. What would you do when all entreaties had failed, your tears had been ignored, and your heart was breaking?

Paul's fellow Christians blessed Paul and sent him on his journey.

Then Paul answered, " 'Why are you weeping and breaking my heart? I am ready not only to be bound, but also to die in Jerusalem for the name of the Lord Jesus.' When he would not be dissuaded, we gave up and said, 'The Lord's will be done'" (21:13-14).

Paul's friends did something all Christians should do. They stated their case the best they could and then blessed Paul even when he determined to ignore their good wisdom. This encourages my heart because it is such a contrast to the actions of some

Christians who attack other Christians who don't agree with them. These are people absolutely convinced they have God's truth in details of doctrine, politics, or behavior and adamantly promote their positions. When other Christians don't agree with them, they criticize, attack, and demean them. There is never, ever any excuse to behave un-Christianly toward anyone, and the Christians from Caesarea showed a better way. They walked sixty-five miles with Paul to Jerusalem, even though they remained convinced he shouldn't go there. "After this, we got ready and went up to Jerusalem. Some of the disciples from Caesarea accompanied us and brought us to the home of Mnason, where we were to stay. He was a man from Cyprus and one of the early disciples" (21:15-16).

How do we make sense of all this? God and the church told Saint Paul not to go to Jerusalem, and he went anyway. Many of us assume that going against the advice of God and Christians ensures disaster. God will zap you for your decision.

We have to skip ahead in the story to find if that was true for Paul. Yes, the predictions were right. He did walk into huge problems and ended up suffering in prison as a result of his trip to Jerusalem.

And God used Paul's imprisonment for great good.

Should we take good advice from God? Absolutely. Does God give up on us if we don't take advice? Of course not. God is our Father and good fathers help their children even when their children do dumb things. God isn't out to hurt us or to get even with us. God is always on our side, even when we are headstrong and set on our own course. Looking at Luke's writings, we see that Paul made his decisions based on a sincere and urgent desire to teach others about Jesus, the Savior. God demonstrated that he knew the heart of Paul and is the God of forgiveness, grace, and blessing.

There is profound comfort in knowing that even when we choose unwisely in our desire to serve God, he is always on our side and able to work things out for good.

Reflect and Discuss

1. The believers at Tyre were guided by the Holy Spirit in warning Paul not to go to Jerusalem. What would the outcome have been if Paul had listened?

2. Do you know Christians who have chosen a course that goes against your advice? Have you been able to bless them and pray for them anyway?

3. Have you wondered if a choice you made was right—then found that God blessed you despite your uncertainty? What does that tell you about God?

CHAPTER 22

SOOTHING
MISUNDERSTANDINGS

(ACTS 21:17-36)

After a year spent gathering funds for destitute Christians in Jerusalem, Paul and eight fellow Christians from churches around the eastern Mediterranean finally arrived in Jerusalem. For Paul, it meant coming home after years of travel to the city where he once lived. He had attended rabbinical school there, preached, and enjoyed fellowship with the members of the first Christian church. It was a city of memories. The others in the group accompanied him through the gates. For most of his fellow travelers it was their first time visiting one of the most famous cities in the world.

James, the brother of Jesus, was then and continued to be the leader of the Jerusalem church and the leader of Jewish Christians across the empire.

About eight years had passed since Paul and James had last seen each other at the Jerusalem Council. That historic meeting, around AD 50, had resulted in the Jerusalem church deciding non-Jews could become Christians solely through faith in Jesus Christ, without first converting to Judaism.

The day after they arrived, Paul and his party met with James and the elders of the Jerusalem church. The church was large—

thousands of new believers had been added over the years—so it is likely many elders gathered to meet with Paul.

Luke wrote in Acts 21 what happened next. The reunion began well.

> When we arrived at Jerusalem, the brothers received us warmly. The next day Paul and the rest of us went to see James, and all the elders were present. Paul greeted them and reported in detail what God had done among the Gentiles through his ministry.
> When they heard this, they praised God. (21:17-20)

Paul reported all that God had done to win Gentiles to Jesus over the past eight years. He told about new churches in Philippi, Thessalonica, Troas, Corinth, and Ephesus. Paul took no credit for himself but "reported in detail what God had done among the Gentiles."

When James and the elders heard this report of miracles, conversions, and great blessings, they praised God. In other words, Paul's report triggered worship and gratitude to God.

However, praise to God quickly turned to expressions of concern about what was going on in those distant cities and not-so-Jewish new churches.

Then they said to Paul: "You see, brother, how many thousands of Jews have believed, and all of them are zealous for the law. They have been informed that you teach all the Jews who live among the Gentiles to turn away from Moses, telling them not to circumcise their children or live according to our customs. What shall we do?" (21:20-22).

What they were worried about was absolutely not true. Paul did not teach Jewish Christians to turn away from the law; instead he told non-Jews they weren't required to keep the law in order to claim salvation.

Abruptly, there was a clash of viewpoints within Christianity.

The elders of the Jerusalem church played some unfair games with Paul to get him to swing to their side.

First they tried a numbers game. In essence they said, "There are thousands of us" (so we must be right).

They tried the success tactic. "Christians in Jerusalem are thoroughly Jewish and very zealous" (so they must be right).

They stooped to using rumors. The new believers "have been informed" that Paul was teaching people to abandon their Jewish practices. (Notice that the informants remained anonymous.)

Luke's writings of this precarious scenario offer a warning to modern Christians. High numbers don't make a crowd correct. Thousands of people spreading a rumor doesn't make it true. Even being zealous doesn't assure the infallibility of disciples.

The elders offered a solution to the mess that had been created by insinuations and misinformation. They suggested Paul join four Jewish Christians who had taken a Nazarite vow, an undertaking to express gratitude to God for a blessing. Throughout a thirty-day period they would consume no meat or wine. As an outward symbol they would not cut their hair. The final seven days were spent in the temple offering sacrifices: lamb (sin offering), ram (peace offering), basket of unleavened bread, cakes of fine flour with oil, meat offering, and drink offering. The men would then shave their heads and burn the hair at the altar.

This was a very expensive ritual because they would lose wages from missed work and spend money on expensive animals to sacrifice. Sometimes those taking the vow sought benefactors to pay their costs.[1] Paul was asked to pay for all four and go along with them to prove that he was still supportive of Jewish practices.

This was asking a lot. Paul had been living in a Greek culture where he taught that these practices were unnecessary. But he agreed to the request in deference to his critics. He seems to have assumed that placating them would satisfy them, so he went along with the idea: "The next day Paul took the men and purified himself along with them. Then he went to the temple to give notice of the date when the days of purification would end and the offering would be made for each of them" (21:26).

The dispute was far from over, however. In fact, it was just getting started.

It appears to have gone well until the last week of the period, when the vow was almost over. Then the real trouble began.

> When the seven days were nearly over, some Jews from the province of Asia saw Paul at the temple. They stirred up the whole crowd and seized him, shouting, "Men of Israel, help us! This is the man who teaches all men everywhere against our people and our law and this place. And besides, he has brought Greeks into the temple area and defiled this holy place." (They had previously seen Trophimus the Ephesian in the city with Paul and assumed that Paul had brought him into the temple area.) (21:27-29)

Trophimus—a convert from Ephesus who was once a pagan silversmith for the goddess Artemis—had joined Paul's team and traveled with him to Jerusalem. They were seen together by Jewish pilgrims visiting Jerusalem for the Pentecost festival. When they saw Paul going in and out of the temple, they assumed that Trophimus was going with him. Non-Jews were strictly forbidden from entering the Jewish temple. Non-Jews were permitted only in the outer "Court of the Gentiles." There was a four-and-a-half-foot barricade blocking their way and a sign threatening death to any foreigners who advanced: "No foreigner may enter within the barricade which surrounds the temple and enclosure. Anyone who is caught doing so will have himself to blame for his ensuing death."[2] The Romans allowed the Jewish authorities to execute anyone who broke this law.

Accused without a chance to defend himself, Paul was assumed to be anti-Jewish. To his critics it proved that Christians were blasphemers and law breakers. What began as a misunderstanding quickly turned into a riot. "The whole city was aroused," wrote Luke, "and the people came running from all directions" (21:30a). Paul was seized and dragged from the temple. It was a dire situation. The people tried to kill him by beating him to death. Did he try to shout out the truth—that he was in the temple to honor Jewish laws and tradition, not to break them? No.

The Roman army had to intervene to stop the riot. The commander of the Roman troops and his officers arrested Paul and had him bound with two chains. When the commander asked the crowd for the story behind the confrontation he "could not get at the truth because of the uproar." He ordered Paul taken into the barracks. Meanwhile the crowd continued shouting for vengeance.

This terrifying scene was not unusual for Paul. He had been the center of other scenes of controversy and violence.

Knowing Jesus' words, Paul tried to appease his Christian brothers and sisters by doing the right thing. He didn't seek revenge; he sought peace. He spoke the truth. He loved the enemy. These are exactly the responses Christ commanded. And yet he was still misunderstood, criticized, and attacked.

Jesus never said that being a Christian would bring less strife and fewer confrontations. In ancient Jerusalem, clashes in culture and differences and disagreements would lead to persecution. Christians would eventually suffer martyrdom by the thousands.

American Christians today enjoy relative peace, but what about Christians around the world? Some historians calculate that there were more Christian martyrs in the twentieth century than in all the previous nineteen centuries combined.[3]

When Christians are falsely accused and misunderstood like Paul, are we justified in getting angry, getting aggressive, and getting even? No. Christians following in Jesus' steps should not seek to arouse further disagreement. Jesus prepared his followers for such occurrences when he taught counterintuitive and revolutionary concepts: "Blessed are you when people insult you, persecute you and falsely say all kinds of evil against you because of me" (Matthew 5:11), and "Love your enemies and pray for those who persecute you" (Matthew 5:44).

Here are encouraging words for times when misunderstanding turns into difficulties: "Do what is right and do not give way to fear" (1 Peter 3:6).

Reflect and Discuss

1. In a comparable situation, what steps would you take based on Paul's actions?

2. Does your Christian faith result in misunderstandings and accusations? If you don't experience conflict, how can you break out of your comfortable Christian community and spend time with unbelievers?

3. Jesus taught that Christians are blessed when they are insulted. How can this truth change your words and behavior?

COUNTING ON GOD'S PLAN

(ACTS 27:1-25)

L ife can feel a lot like getting shoved out to sea on an inner tube. What starts out fun turns into fear. What should be simple becomes complicated. What begins as a great day turns into one of the worst days of your life. Rather than pleasant bobbing and floating, you may feel cut adrift—or, worse, as though you're sinking fast, alone in icy ocean waters.

Why would God allow this to happen? When a dream is shattered, a relationship crumbles, sickness comes, a life ends—we want to know where God was and why tragedy occurred. Christians, especially, may feel abandoned, believing that faith exempts us from the most devastating problems of life. We desire reward for our trust, praise, obedience, and commitment. Some believers come out of horrendous experiences feeling that God has broken his end of the bargain.

Paul had experienced more than his share of troubles in life. In Jerusalem, he had been the target of two assassination plots. He had argued his case before the Sanhedrin to no avail. He was tried before Herod and spent two years in prison. He was next tried by Festus and requested audience with Caesar as a Roman citizen.

As if all of these discouragements and disasters weren't enough, he was about to find out what literal stormy waters were.

The journey started one day in October AD 60 when he boarded a sailboat at the Mediterranean port of Caesarea. This was no pleasure cruise. He had been accused of being "a troublemaker, stirring up riots among the Jews all over the world" (Acts 24:5). Now he was a prisoner of the Romans, bound with shackles and under military guard. Paul was on his way to Rome for the trial of his life.

> When it was decided that we would sail for Italy, Paul and some other prisoners were handed over to a centurion named Julius, who belonged to the Imperial Regiment. We boarded a ship from Adramyttium about to sail for ports along the coast of the province of Asia, and we put out to sea. Aristarchus, a Macedonian from Thessalonica, was with us. (27:1-2)

It was dangerously late in the shipping season for this trip; early winter storms were always a possibility. Perhaps that's why there wasn't a ship sailing directly to Rome. This was a coastal transport headed along the shoreline rather than across the sea. They would have to switch to another vessel at another port.

Paul was blessed to have company—his longtime companion and biographer, Luke, and Aristarchus, a fellow Christian from Macedonia who had been journeying with him the last several years. How did these two get tickets on a prisoner transport? Upper-class Roman prisoners were allowed to bring their slaves along with them when going to the appellate court. It's possible Paul's two friends became his "slaves" so he wouldn't have to travel alone.

There is no way any of them could have known what was ahead or how hard this voyage would become. But life is like that. We never know if a routine journey will end in relaxation or catastrophe. A new job could be the beginning of a great career or a tragic disappointment. A date could lead to marriage or a broken relationship.

For a Christian the uncertainties of life's journeys are tempered by the presence of God. Paul was not alone. The Spirit of God boarded with him. The Lord of heaven was watching over him. Everything else was uncertain, but Jesus' care was guaranteed— for Paul and for us.

The voyage began well. The ship traveled north up the coast of Israel to the port of Sidon. The Roman officer named Julius belonged to the prestigious Imperial Regiment. He took a liking to Paul—perhaps because Paul was educated and seemingly upper-class with his two "slaves." So Julius released Paul on his own recognizance to visit friends in the city of Sidon.

After they left Sidon the headwinds began to pick up. The ship no longer hugged the coast but sailed into the open sea on the north side of Cyprus. The centurion moved his prisoners to a larger ship at the port of Myra—a grain ship from Alexandria in Egypt making the last run before winter to deliver a large shipment to Rome. Egypt was then the breadbasket of the Roman Empire.

It was slow going for the large, cumbersome vessel that was unable to easily tack into the headwind. They made little progress. As the days ticked toward November, the journey became more and more dangerous. The shipping season was coming to an end. Now the possibility of storms would increase, perilous for any sailing vessel. Whenever possible they pulled into ports, hoping that weather conditions would soon improve, but they did not. They kept getting worse.

"The winds were against us," wrote Luke in Acts 27:4. You know what that's like. No matter how hard you try, you cannot move ahead. You plan and work and pray and hope to get traction, but you go nowhere. The winds are constantly against you. They stop you from going where you want to go and they keep blowing you off course until you are tired and desperate.

Paul and crew docked at Fair Havens, near the town of Lasea, but it was a place unsafe to winter in. We know where and when Paul's difficulties happened from Luke's detailed geography and reference to the Jewish "Fast" (Yom Kippur, the Day of Atonement). Time had been lost, and sailing had already become dangerous. Paul warned the crew and his captor, "Men, I can see that our voyage is going to be disastrous and bring great loss to ship and cargo, and to our own lives also" (27:10).

Paul was a man of experience and knew what he was talking about. He may have had more frequent sailor miles than anyone on the ship. This was at least his eleventh crossing of the Mediterranean, which meant more than 3,000 miles at sea. Guided by the Holy Spirit, he spoke frankly of the potential disaster ahead if they continued. But the centurion ignored Paul's advice and—after consulting with the captain and owner of the ship—decided to make a run for a bigger and better harbor at Phoenix on the island of Crete. "When a gentle south wind began to blow, they thought they had obtained what they wanted; so they weighed anchor and sailed along the shore of Crete" (27:13).

At first it looked like Paul was wrong and everybody else was right; however, a few days of good weather doesn't mean that the rest of the journey will be easy. We hope and pray for the best. We welcome the blue skies, south wind, and easy travel. Still, we need to be prepared for anything.

The weather suddenly changed and they were caught in a hurricane. Imagine being caught in a massive storm on the open sea. What happened next must have been a living nightmare. They lost all control. There was no navigation. They simply let the storm control the ship. The sailors were barely able to pull the lifeboat they were dragging up onto the deck. Fearing the ship was about to fall apart, the crew put ropes around the hull to hold it together.

Many days passed with thick clouds and roaring wind. There was no sight of the sun, moon, or stars. They couldn't determine if they were being driven north, south, east, or west. Afraid that they were nearing the coast of North Africa, where so many ships had been sunk by the sandbars and rocks, they threw out anchors to slow the ship. They even threw the cargo and ship's rigging overboard to lighten the vessel. Finally they "gave up all hope of being saved" (27:20).

Maybe you've been there. You've done everything you know to do. Nothing works and there appears to be no way out of your difficulty. You are totally controlled by a violent storm raging around you and you just give up.

Then came courage. The man who knew Jesus spoke, the one no one would listen to before, the prisoner headed to trial in Rome, the Christian—Paul. The men were weak from going without food. They were cold, wet, and without a shred of hope.

> "Now I urge you to keep up your courage, because not one of you will be lost; only the ship will be destroyed. Last night an angel of the God whose I am and whom I serve stood beside me and said, 'Do not be afraid, Paul. You must stand trial before Caesar; and God has graciously given you the lives of all who sail with you.' So keep up your courage, men, for I have faith in God that it will happen just as he told me. Nevertheless, we must run aground on some island." (Acts 27:22-26)

Paul was convinced of God's calling and purpose in his life. God had something for him to do and would save him from the storm, although things looked bleak. He had faith in God and called the men to courage and faith.

Are you convinced that God has a plan for you? Do you know God's purpose for you? Are you convinced there is more for you to do for God? Take courage that he will get you through every storm—no matter how violent, hurtful, and destructive—until you've accomplished what you have been called to do.

Paul was a strong Christian, an apostle, a saint. Even so, life got tough. For a while it seemed that everything went wrong. Through his life story we see that followers of Jesus are not excused from contrary winds. We too get blown off course. Don't be surprised by pain, problems, difficulty, disappointment, or hurricane-force winds. Take courage and hold on to hope. God has plans for you. Although you may not feel his presence when you're out at sea and pitching helplessly in the hurricane, God promises to be present and to get us back on track with his plans when the winds subside.

Reflect and Discuss

1. What evidence was there that Paul, although suffering, also experienced God's blessings?

2. Has there been a time in your life when you couldn't see God's purpose for you while you were entangled in difficulty? What happened?

3. How do you prepare for the stormy seas? How did Paul prepare?

CHAPTER 24

USING OUR TIME FOR HIM

(ACTS 28:11-31)

Paul had a dream of going to Rome, the capital city in the greatest empire of his world. A widely traveled man, he had visited Jerusalem, Damascus, Ephesus, and Athens, but Rome was in a league all its own. He was a Roman citizen who had heard stories all his life about the Seven Hills, the Forum, and the Circus Maximus.

But behind his patriotism and curiosity, something deeper compelled him. He knew that swaying Romans to faith in Jesus was key to winning a highly significant portion of the world to his Lord. Imagine his heart beating faster as he finally caught his first glimpse of this magnificent city. He had been shipwrecked on Malta, laid up during three months of winter, stuck on a boat en route to the city of his dreams. When he finally arrived in Puteoli, the commercial seaport for the city of Rome, Paul and the other travelers found fellow Christians waiting for them. The church of Jesus was spreading so quickly that Christians could be found almost everywhere. This must have thrilled Paul's heart, for it was evidence that the small seed Jesus had planted in Jerusalem had taken root and was spreading on its own. It was now possible to meet devoted followers of Jesus in the most unlikely of places.

Soon they started walking the Appian Way toward the great city. This was (and is) one of the most wonderful roads in the world—straight and strong. It was the main highway to the capital of the empire. Paul's excitement must have been growing. And then God gave him a spectacular surprise: Christians from Rome came to welcome him. Some walked forty-three miles to a market town called the Forum of Appius and others walked thirty-three miles to a town called Three Taverns. Paul was used to going where there were no believers and starting from scratch. The church of Jesus was expanding so far and fast that it was ahead of him. Those who came to welcome him were the recipients of Paul's longest and most theological letter that we call the book of Romans. It is no wonder that "at the sight of these men Paul thanked God and was encouraged" (28:15b). For years he had endured the harassment of many who criticized and discouraged him, but here were believers coming to bless and encourage him. After all he had been through, friendship and fellowship were exactly what he needed.

Finally he saw the city of his dreams, the place God had promised to take him, the center of Western civilization—Rome.

The Roman authorities allowed Paul to await trial under house arrest rather than in a Roman jail. While he did have a Roman soldier chained to his right wrist, he also had a surprising amount of freedom.

For three days Paul rested and got settled and then was ready to tackle the challenges before him. He invited the leaders of the Jewish community in Rome to his home to give his explanation of what had happened.

When they arrived, Paul made three points in his speech: (1) He did nothing wrong against the Jews or the Jewish religion. (2) The Romans never convicted him of any crime. (3) He had no grudge against Jews; in fact, he was a loyal Jew himself. He explained to them why he had come to Rome in chains, as a criminal. Their answer surprised him.

> They replied, "We have not received any letters from Judea concerning you, and none of the brothers who have come from

there has reported or said anything bad about you. But we want to hear what your views are, for we know that people everywhere are talking against this sect." (28:21-22)

Paul seems to have assumed they knew all the accusations that had been leveled against him, but they knew nothing. This was good news because the thinking of the Jewish people had not been biased before Paul had a chance to teach. The Roman Jews had heard about Jesus, his teachings, and the church, and they wanted to hear more.

Notice that in his first conversation with the Jewish leaders Paul made no mention of Jesus at all. He didn't scare them away or polarize them before he could give a full explanation of the gospel. As he often did, Paul used common sense and sensitivity.

Paul was always willing to meet anyone, anywhere, anytime to talk about Jesus Christ and the salvation from sin that he offered. A date was set for people from the synagogue of Rome to come and listen to Paul talk about Jesus.

They arranged to meet Paul on a certain day and came in even larger numbers to the place where he was staying. From morning until evening he explained and declared to them the kingdom of God and tried to convince them about Jesus from the law of Moses and from the prophets.

Picture the meeting at the house where Paul was staying. It could have been a large Roman villa with space for hundreds or more. The place was packed. Paul, handcuffed to a Roman soldier, taught from early morning until after sunset. He delivered a one-day course on Christian faith, arguing that the messianic prophecies of the Hebrew Scriptures were fulfilled in the birth, life, death, and resurrection of Jesus.

Reactions were mixed.

Some were convinced by what he said, but others would not believe. They disagreed among themselves and began to leave after Paul had made this final statement:

"The Holy Spirit spoke the truth to your forefathers when he said through Isaiah the prophet:

" 'Go to this people and say,
   "You will be ever hearing but never understanding;
   you will be ever seeing but never perceiving."
For this people's heart has become calloused;
   they hardly hear with their ears,
   and they have closed their eyes.
Otherwise they might see with their eyes,
   hear with their ears,
   understand with their hearts
and turn, and I would heal them.'
   "Therefore I want you to know that God's salvation has
been sent to the Gentiles, and they will listen!" (28:25-28)

Paul gave it his all, allowing everyone to make a choice. When
he saw the antagonism of those who rejected the gospel, he para-
phrased a warning from the prophet Isaiah (Isaiah 6:9-10). It was
his coup de grâce, delivered after it was clear that some individuals remained inflexible and hard-hearted despite his persuasive
message. As usual, Paul was passionate. He thrilled to welcome
new Christians into the church and yearned for those who rejected
Jesus to change their minds. He also recognized the reality of personal choice. As a Christian, his job was to communicate the
truth, joy, peace, and hope of Jesus, and then allow God to change
hearts.

The remainder of Acts 28 details his activities during the continuing house arrest. Paul did not receive a speedy trial. He had
already spent almost three years in trials, jail, and shipwrecks
before arriving in Rome for his appeal to Caesar, and the waiting
was to continue. The last two sentences in the book of Acts read,
"For two whole years Paul stayed there in his own rented house
and welcomed all who came to see him. Boldly and without hindrance he preached the kingdom of God and taught about the
Lord Jesus Christ" (28:30-31).

When I try to put myself in Paul's place, I feel enormous frus-
tration. It's hard to wait, especially when there is work to be done
and goals to achieve. And Paul was an activist. He loved to travel.
He was an entrepreneur who started churches and took on causes.

This man, above all others, didn't seem wired for waiting. Yet he used these two years to accomplish great things for God.

Between AD 61 and AD 63, while still under house arrest, Paul wrote four books of the New Testament. They are now called the "Prison Epistles" (Ephesians, Philippians, Colossians, and Philemon). They are among my favorite books of the Bible because they express Christian truth along with Paul's unfailing faith, hope, and joy. For a guy in prison, Paul seemed to be a very happy, productive man. Imagine if he had missed that opportunity to write those letters. God even turned jail into good for Paul—and for us.

In addition to his writing, he used the site of his house arrest as a hub for Christian teaching. Even while limited in physical freedom, he continued growing the church and changing the world. Acts 28:31 reports, "Boldly and without hindrance he preached the kingdom of God and taught about the Lord Jesus Christ." Picture Paul chained to different guards on changing shifts, day after day. Surely he spoke to them about Jesus and the eternal life he offers. How many zealous new Christians infiltrated the Praetorian Guard in Caesar's palace because of Paul's tireless evangelism? Picture Paul teaching believers and unbelievers who came to visit him every day, Paul preaching to the Roman church members who came to his home for services, Paul talking about the Messiah Jesus to Nero when his appeal to the emperor was finally heard.

Do you hate to wait? Does it seem like a waste of time and life to be stuck between jobs, mired in a difficult relationship, living with a serious illness, or wishing for a child of your own? Even if you're not actually serving jail time, it can seem like you are in prison.

When God puts you on hold for two weeks, two years, or two decades, never consider the time wasted. Always count it as time to serve. No matter the circumstances of our lives and the impatience we feel for the next great thing, we have—like Paul—a constant, God-given opportunity to live for and like Jesus every day of our lives.

Reflect and Discuss

1. Much of Acts details Paul's passion for evangelism and his determination to tell the good news, whatever the cost. On the other hand, we read much about Paul waiting—in prison, on ships, and for the right time. Patience is a characteristic required by God. How did Paul balance his impatience with patience?

2. Have you been called to be patient when you felt impatient?

3. Can you name times that have felt wasted? In retrospect, can you name what you have gleaned from those times?

EPILOGUE

A cts begins with Jesus' ascension to heaven in AD 29 and ends with Paul in prison in AD 61. It starts with 120 followers of Jesus in Jerusalem and ends with tens of thousands of Christians in countless churches across the Roman Empire and beyond.

I love this book. I love the story it tells of the stunning explosion of growth in the church, the amazing work of the Holy Spirit, the dogged passion of Paul, and the supernatural ways people came to faith in Jesus. Most of all, I love the challenge offered to believers through Luke's writing: to continue the growth of God's church in ensuing generations. His message is directed to us—and into the future.

The book of Acts is a vivid record of how the Christian church changed the world—not by force but by love. The new followers of the martyred Jesus lived Christianly among pagans, started new churches, shared good news with all kinds of people, and risked their lives in the process. Two hundred and fifty years after Acts was completed, a majority of Romans professed faith in Jesus, and Christianity had spread across the empire. Two thousand years later, the church of Jesus Christ is everywhere in the world, the largest religion in history, and the hope of billions.

What happened to Paul? To answer that question we must look beyond the book of Acts. Paul expected to be released from prison, according to what he wrote to the Philippians.

> I know that through your prayers and the help given by the
> Spirit of Jesus Christ, what has happened to me will turn out for

my deliverance. I eagerly expect and hope that I will in no way be ashamed, but will have sufficient courage so that now as always Christ will be exalted in my body, whether by life or by death. For to me, to live is Christ and to die is gain. If I am to go on living in the body, this will mean fruitful labor for me. Yet what shall I choose? I do not know! I am torn between the two: I desire to depart and be with Christ, which is better by far; but it is more necessary for you that I remain in the body. Convinced of this, I know that I will remain, and I will continue with all of you for your progress and joy in the faith, so that through my being with you again your joy in Christ Jesus will overflow on account of me. (Philippians 1:19-26)

History and tradition tell us that the prayers of the Philippian church were answered and Paul was set free. He traveled for another two years, was rearrested, tried in Rome, convicted, and sentenced to death. Because he was a Roman citizen, he could not be crucified. Paul was beheaded as a martyr for Jesus Christ in AD 64.

The book of Acts is finished. Or is it? No, the book is still being written. You are in it. As long as his followers are telling the good news of Jesus, the story goes on. This is your story, the church's story, and Jesus' story intertwined. The church of Jesus Christ continues to change the world.

NOTES

Preface

1. See www.adherents.com/Religions_By_Adherents.html

1. Moving Forward

1. The third book of the New Testament, called "The Gospel According to Luke," is the longest and most detailed of the four New Testament accounts of Jesus' life, birth, death, and resurrection.

2. Seeking God's Will

1. The Greek word used is *proskartereō.*

3. Welcoming the Spirit

1. John R. W. Stott, *The Message of Acts* (Downers Grove, Ill.: InterVarsity Press, 1994), 69.
2. The word used is *gleukos,* which means "sweet new wine" in Greek.

9. Telling the Truth to God

1. In the hot Middle East, bodies were and are buried very quickly. It is possible that the body was simply moved to a nearby

cave for formal burial later. It probably wasn't buried in the ground as we usually do in America.

10. Enduring Persecution

1. John R. W. Stott, *The Message of Acts* (Downers Grove, Ill.: InterVarsity Press, 1994), 119.

2. Ibid.

3. Chuck Colson in Nina Shea's book, *In the Lion's Den* (Nashville: Broadman & Holman Publishers, 1997), ix.

4. Andrew Black and Craig Bird, "The Risk of Faith," *FaithWorks* (July/August 1999): 17-20. *Faith Works* was published by Associated Baptist Press. Used by permission.

11. Organizing to Grow

1. John R. W. Stott, *The Message of Acts* (Downers Grove, Ill.: InterVarsity Press, 1994), 120.

2. William J. Larkin, Jr., *Acts* (Downers Grove, Ill.: InterVarsity Press, 1995), 98.

14. Imitating Jesus

1. F. F. Bruce, *The Book of the Acts,* The New International Commentary on the New Testament (Grand Rapids, Mich.: Eerdmans, 1988), 291-92.

16. Aligning with God's Vision

1. Pisidian Antioch synagogue (compare Acts 13:14 and Galatians 4:13).

2. Steve Gertz, *History & Biography Newsletter,* April 2, 2005.

3. Christopher J. H. Wright, "An Upside-Down World," *Christianity Today* 51, no. 1 (January 2007).

17. Persevering in the Worst Circumstances

1. William Barclay, *The Acts of the Apostles* (Louisville: Westminster John Knox Press, 2003), 123.

18. Confronting Challenges with Hope

1. William Barclay, *The Acts of the Apostles* (Louisville: Westminster John Knox Press, 2003), 136.
2. Jim Collins, *Good to Great* (New York, N.Y.: HarperBusiness, 2001), 13.

19. Modeling the Way, Not Arguing

1. Jesus said, "I am the way and the truth and the life" (John 14:6).

22. Soothing Misunderstandings

1. William Barclay, *The Acts of the Apostles* (Louisville: Westminster John Knox Press, 2003), 155-156.
2. John R. W. Stott, *The Message of Acts* (Downers Grove, Ill.: InterVarsity Press, 1994), 334.
3. Chuck Colson in Nina Shea's book, *In the Lion's Den* (Nashville: Broadman & Holman Publishers, 1997), ix.